PEAKLAND PICKINGS

Stories and Characters of the Peak District

Neville T. Sharpe

CHURNET VALLEY BOOKS
Leek, Staffordshire: 01538 399033
Publishing Local History
Specialist Bookseller of Ornithology and Biography

©Neville T. Sharpe and Churnet Valley Books 1999
ISBN 1 897949 51 0

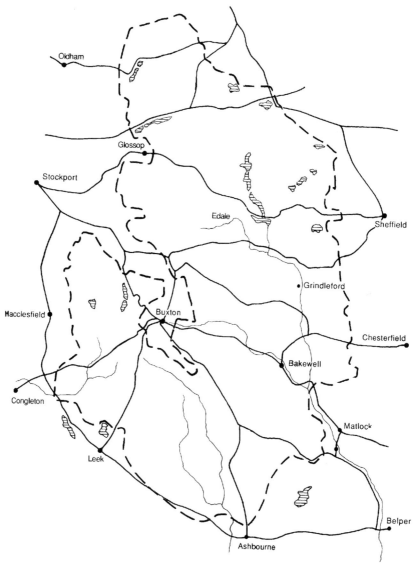

CONTENTS

VIEW from within PEAKE HOLE near CASTLETON, DERBYSHIRE

From Chantrey's Peak Scenery 1886

INTRODUCTION

Every weekend in better weather people flood out of the Potteries into beautiful Dovedale and the surrounding countryside, and who can blame them? Folks in Manchester and Sheffield will tell you, "Derbyshire's great," and so it is, on a glorious day when the skylark sings on high, the heather is coming into bloom on the high moors and in the limestone country a profusion of wild flowers carpet the ground. They might well have something less complimentary to say if they visited in winter on a day with the snow sweeping horizontally across the landscape and scarcely a living creature to be seen except perhaps a few sheep huddled in the shelter of a dry stone wall.

Daniel Defoe in his travels during the 1720s described the Peak of Derbyshire as a "A Waste and a Houling Wilderness." To this day, anyone struggling through a blizzard over Cold Harbour Moor at the Summit of the Snake Pass or trying to make their way from Ashbourne to Buxton along the A515 might be tempted to agree with him, despite being cosseted within the heated interiors of their horseless carriages. Try for a moment, to imagine making the same journeys on foot or horseback over 200 years ago when the roads were mere tracks, with only an old sack wrapped round your shoulders to keep out the worst of the elements.

On the other hand, pause for a while and imagine lying on a bank of crowberry in some remote clough off the Derwent Valley, with the sunlight streaming down, idly watching a buzzard circling high above and listening to the plaintive piping of a golden plover on a distant hillock; or beside some stream in limestone country watching the trout rise to take a fly. Clearly Mr Defoe visited at the wrong time of year.

In his 'A Description of the Country from 30 to 40 Miles Round Manchester,' published in 1795, J. Aiken describes the local climate:

'The mountainous part of Derbyshire is distinguished from the rest by the greater quantity of rain which falls in it. At Chatsworth which is by no means the highest part, about 33 inches of rain have been found to fall annually at a medium. The High Peak is particularly liable to very violent storms in which the rain descends in torrents, so as frequently to occasion great ravages of the lands: it is also subject to very high winds. These causes, together with the elevation of the country render it cold, so that vegetation is backward and unkindly. Some kinds of grain will not grow at all in the Peak, and others seldom ripen till very late in the year...'

This accurate description will be readily recognised and here we have the reason for the siting of the ancient villages by our Saxon forebears. Almost all of them are placed on hillsides, well clear of some sudden downpour. People living in close contact with the elements knew better than to build in places where their homes could be swept away by some sudden deluge. The development of the practice of building in unsuitable, flood prone locations had to wait until the Industrial Revolution when rows of cottages were

Raven's Tor, Dovedale.

Lion's Head Rock, Dovedale.

constructed in valley bottoms, next to water powered mills so that the hands could be close to their work.

From the Journeys of Celia Fiennes, 1697, we receive yet another description:
"All Derbyshire is full of steep hills, and nothing but the peakes of hills as thick one by another is seen in most of the County which are very steepe which makes travelling tedious, and the miles long, you see neither hedge nor tree but only low drye stone walls round some ground, else its only hills and dales as thick as you can imagine, but tho' the surface of the earth looks barren yet those hills are impregnated with rich Marbles, Stones, Metals, Iron and Copper and Coale mines in their bowells, from whence we may see the wisdom and benignitye of our greate Creator to make up the deficiency of a place by an equivalent as also the diversity of the Creation which encreaseth its Beauty."

This is one aspect of the district that has seen tremendous change. Old photographs reveal a landscape almost bare of trees, whereas today any steep sided valley which is not grazed is usually covered with them. I suspect that the former lack of trees had something to do with the fact that folks needed all the fuel they could lay their hands on to survive a Peakland winter. As one old chap put it to me as he sawed away in his yard. "I allus say that nowt's too good to burn." It would not require too many folks holding to this philosophy to clear every vestige of a tree from the landscape.

Exactly what area do we mean by the High Peak? Should it be restricted to Derbyshire? Or does it include that portion of Cheshire north of the Etherow that was transferred to Derbyshire, or the parts of Derbyshire around Marple Bridge which have gradually been moved in the opposite direction?

The ancient Forest of Peak might give us one possible answer. The bounds of the Forest of Peak as set forth in the forest pleas held in 1286 were as follows:
"The metes and bounds of the Forest of Peak begin on the south at the New Place of Goyt, and thence by the river Goyt as far as the river Etherow; and so by the river Etherow to Longley Croft at Longdenhead; thence by a certain footpath to the head of Derwent; and from the head of Derwent to a place called Mythomstede (Mytham Bridge), and from Mytham Bridge to the river Bradwell; and from the river Bradwell as far as a certain place called Hucklow to the great dell (cave?) of Hazelbache; and from that dell as far as Little Hucklow; and from Hucklow to the brook of Tideswell; and so to the river Wye; and from the Wye ascending up to Buxton, and so on to the New Place of Goyt."

Most of this outline can be traced out easily to this day, but unfortunately it cuts off much of the White Peak which would never do. The Forest of Peak had three divisions; Longdendale, Hopedale and the Compagna, and all three met at Edale Cross. The present cross seems too well preserved to have lasted so well in such an exposed place; presumably it is not the only example to have stood on that spot.

The area of the Peak District National Park might seem a useful guide, stretching as it does across county boundaries but here again several of the larger towns and villages are not included. The inhabitants of Hayfield, Chapel-en-le-Frith and Buxton for instance might have something to say if told they did not live within the Peak.

The etymology of the word 'Peak' is not very helpful. There is plenty of high land but very few hills which could merit the description 'peak'. Lose Hill is perhaps the best example but Pikenaze; Peaknaze; Win Hill Pike; Lantern Pike; Eccles Pike can give the impression of rising to a high point when viewed from the right position.

From the Tribal Hidage, a tribute list drawn up in Mercian times, we learn that a tribe known as the Pecsaetan (Peak dwellers) had 1200 hides of land in what is now north-west Derbyshire, parts of Staffordshire and Cheshire adjoining. This is generally regarded as the origin of the name of the district and as the Tribal Hidage may have been written as early as 660 A.D. it is not unreasonable that the district should have thus gained its name just as most of our towns and villages have names with Anglo-Saxon origins.

A few hundred years later in 923 AD when King Alfred the Great's son, Edward the Elder, at the head of the West Saxons and Mercians was reclaiming England from the Danes, we learn from the Anglo-Saxon Chronicle that "Edward built a town at Badecanwyllan (Bakewell) in Peacland, and fortified it with a castle."

These are weighty matters best left to those who have just transferred from the Sun to the Guardian. If politicians can alter our ancient county boundaries at will, without reference to, or any obvious benefit to the public, why should we not make a foray into the Staffordshire Roches, or across the Derwent, if it results in a story worth the telling? Should any misguided soul have the nerve to write and tell me that I have included a tale from outside the Peak, I will make a paper dart with it and launch it from the top of Kinder Downfall.

Of course, those born within the Peak know where it is without the need for academic cogitations. At this point it must definitely be pointed out that you have to be born within the Peak to be totally accepted as a member of the local community. You could move into a village as a babe in arms and live there till you are ninety, but be under no misapprehension, at your funeral there will always be someone there to say, "E were a grand chap, but 'e werna born 'ere; come from round Rawtenstall by all accounts."

This odd state of affairs has produced certain choleric characters who seem to revel in funerals, and who, if they are unable to attend in person, will read the obituary column in the local paper with relish before making appropriate comments such as; "I see owd so and so has dropped off his perch. 'E won't be missed."

Most of the history taught at school was that of the rich and powerful, with the stress laid on their accomplishments and their shortcomings carefully glossed over, or even completely omitted. You may find this error rectified occasionally in the stories that follow. The lives and exertions of lesser folks were not considered worthy of mention, although their collective efforts can only have been vital to the growth of the nation.

Regrettably, there are those at large within the community, often of an academic bent, who suffer from the delusion that our local history belongs to them. In an effort to overcome such arrogance I therefore take every opportunity to reveal what little I know to anyone who shows some interest.

The following stories are based on historical events, even if the details have been improved at each telling. The Peak has never been a wealthy part of England (with perhaps the exception of the fortunes made from cotton during the nineteenth century) and the struggle to survive its inhospitable climate in the past has produced some very hardy individuals every bit as tough as their environment, so it is hardly surprising if many stories are concerned with violent events and some desperate characters. One could be excused for gathering the impression from the 'media' that we live in lawless times. It is not all that long ago that highwaymen and footpads were at large along turnpikes and country lanes, the bodies of malefactors swung from gibbets, riots were commonplace, and strangers were stoned on sight in many an out of the way village.

Walking through odd corners of the Peak I am driven to the conclusion that it is possible to learn more talking to a farmer over a five barred gate than from a host of academics; not all that surprising really, many farmers have lived on a particular farm all their lives as did their fathers and grandfathers before them. They are the possessors of information passed down through the generations that rarely appears on maps or in writing; the names of fields and the reasons for them for instance.

A Milldale farmer told me, "This bridge down the lane, the so called Viator's Bridge, isn't called that locally at all. I don't know who dreamed up the name. We have always known it as the packhorse bridge. The packhorses carrying copper ore from the Ecton mines used to come down this lane and cross the Dove by the bridge."

Another very old character in the Upper Derwent Valley told me how they used to harvest the hay years ago. The fields were far too steep to use a haywain so they always used sledges. He also told me about the conduit which carries water from the River Alport into the Derwent Reservoir. Before the conduit was put to use, he and other young men in the valley would cycle to the entrance, leave the cycles there and walk through on their way to the Snake Inn for an evenings entertainment, returning by the same route.

One word of warning, whatever you do, should you be fortunate enough to join in conversation with one of these sterling fellows, for goodness sake don't try to tell them anything. You must remember they are the experts on their own stamping ground.

Fail to follow this advice and you will see a sudden change in demeanour and you may well be told to 'be off' with a few good old Anglo-Saxon expletives to send you on your way rejoicing. Finally, whatever you do, don't produce one of those pocket tape recorders, that is unless you want your informant to clam up, or worse still, part your hair with the knob end of a stick.

Some of these chaps have a rather dour sense of humour. They will cheerfully lean over a gate smoking a pipe of tobacco while the professor and his students dig up the field in quest of some Roman Road, or ancient burial site. When, days later, the site is eventually discovered right under the gate, he will make some such comment as, "My grandfather always said it was just here."

"Why on earth didn't you tell us sooner?"

"Well, tha never asked."

Listening carefully has often put me on the trail of some antiquity; the origin of a place name; the site of some long lost industry, or perhaps best of all from my nonagenarian friends, an insight into everyday life before most of us were born.

Time and again they make the same complaint, "They keep coming round to ask me about it, but when I tell them they don't believe me. Their eyes glass over as soon as I tell them what they don't want to hear." Or best of all, "Somebody should write it all down before it's forgotten." Of course when I do, the next comment is, "I towd you that story." "Ah, but have I got it reet?" "More or less."

What greater accolade could one wish for? Some of these types like nothing better than to spin a tall tale for the benefit of the credulous visitor so it might be a good idea to do a spot of checking on the more unlikely tales. This might not be as easy as you think. Once something appears in print, others rush to believe it and before you know what is happening, it is being quoted as gospel. I have read with interest how the village of Simmondley got its name from a Saxon called Simond who is listed in the Domesday Book. It might be true that the name is derived from Simond's Ley, or field, but it certainly does not appear in Domesday Book. Neither is there a word of truth in the assertion that the ancestors of the numerous Booths who live in Charlesworth and thereabouts had an ancestor mentioned in that ancient tome.

I make no claim to have rooted out all these well entrenched errors but wherever possible I have gone back to sources such as the Quarter Sessions records and newspapers of the time. The golden rule when reading newspapers is to believe nothing below the date, and to check that carefully. The same strictures apply to older newspapers, possibly more so, although one thing that must be said in their defence is that the standard of English was generally better.

You have to understand how local newspapers function to realise how these errors appear. Firstly there is the policy of the deliberate mistake. No matter how careful you are to give the press the details of your late relative, when his obituary notice appears they will certainly have given the number of the house for his age or some similar error.

The object of the exercise is to stir up the populace to make such comments as, "He were never 76; we went to school together." or "I don't remember 'im working at Cronshaw's Mill, and I were there for thirty years."

Imagine for a moment the scene in the office when young Inkster is given the job of reporting on the Highlow Well Dressings. Having already learned the ropes he gets out the files on previous well dressings and rehashes them without bothering to check the facts. The nearest he will get to the Well Dressings is to have a swift half in the Devonshire Arms. This is why if you compare the reports on any local event you find the same nonsense repeated year after year, ad infinitum.

Thus you will read once again such utter baloney as 'The Highlow Well Dressings are held in September because then heather is in bloom." If such pressing matters keep you awake at night, you will find the true reason in the article on the Old Wakes.

It is often possible to learn more by putting on a pair of stout boots and walking over the ground than by reading about it. You can meet someone who fills in a few vital details and is glad of a good listener. A typical example of this is the Engine Pit at Chisworth. According to others who have put pen to paper it gained its name because it was the first pit in the district to have a steam engine installed. After talking to local people whose ancestors were colliers in the very pit a totally different story emerges. Let me try to put it in the words of my informant.

"They brought the engine down the brow from Charlesworth and folks thought the road might collapse under the weight because the land underneath is honeycombed with old mine workings. None of the coal pits had a steam engine, they were all worked by hand. The engine went into Holehouse Mill and the pit was so close that when the engine was running its vibrations could be felt underground and this was why it got the name of the Engine Pit. I wish they would get it right."

I am frequently asked how it is possible to do research into English local history while living in Australia. In some ways it is much easier because in Australia there is open access for the public to university libraries and I have received every assistance, whereas, alas, in Britain you might easily get the impression that the Official Secrets Act applies. On the other hand I have always received unstinting help from members of the Derbyshire Records Office, the Derbyshire Library Service, and if any particular section had to be singled out it must be the ladies who work in the Local Studies Library at Matlock.

Naturally, I cannot finish this brief introduction without a word of thanks to all those farmers, plasterers, bakers, joiners, policemen, accountants, quarrymen, stonemasons, brickmakers, rope piecers, cobblers, cotton operatives, millwrights, and all the other working men and women who have both educated and entertained me with their memories. I only hope that I have done justice to their stories.

Edale Cross, marking the junction of the three divisions of the Forest of Peak.

Packhorse Bridge, Milldale.

PEAKLAND PICKINGS

The Case Is Altered!

At Sparrowpit is a tavern called the 'Wanted Inn'. Over the years the name has altered several times and at one time it was known as 'The Case Is Altered.' The story behind this unusual name is as follows.

One night in this pub a farmer and a solicitor were in deep discussion when the farmer said, *"I have been having a lot of trouble recently with cows straying onto my land. Do you think I would have a case for compensation against the owner of the cows?"*

"Certainly," replied the solicitor, *"Whose cows are they?"*

"Yours," said the farmer.

"Ah, I'm afraid if they were my cows, then the case is altered."

Besom and the Grey Mare

Firstly, a cautionary tale which is a prime example of how a story can be improved out of all recognition until all semblance of fact disappears and folks are still quite happy to believe anything written down in printer's ink.

Charlesworth may seem a quiet spot, but it has known some uproarious incidents, the story of Besom Sam and his grey mare being just one of the better known. In the usual version of this yarn which has gained considerable credence, Sam Higginbottom was a man overfond of a drink and the local Vicar decided to attempt to reform him. His intended method of conversion was most unusual, taking the form of a wager, the conditions of which were as follows. The Vicar and Besom Sam were to contest a race from Charlesworth to Stockport Market, Sam to be mounted on his old grey mare and the Vicar on his blood hunter. If the Vicar won, then Sam would have to attend church every Sunday for a twelvemonth which would doubtless have come as an unpleasant shock, whilst if Sam turned out to be the victor, then the Vicar would have to settle his beer bill for the year, an even greater shock. The Vicar would have to be very confident of success to take on the risk of the expense involved in slaking Sam's thirst.

If the Vicar had proved victorious, the bet would have been long forgotten. Needless to say, it is claimed that Sam was first to arrive at Stockport Market and the Vicar had to stump up. When Sam and his horse returned to Charlesworth, an unruly crowd was waiting for them. The pair were carried bodily into the village pub and both horse and rider drank deeply at the Vicar's expense. The wild carousing went on until the company were in such a state that some of them led the horse upstairs and put it to bed in an inebriated condition. Next morning the horse was in fine fettle which was more than could be said for the bed. According to some, the pub was called the Grey Mare Inn from that date.

St John's Church, Charlesworth.

Heading east up the old packhorse route, with the Abbey Brook to the left.

It is nothing out of the ordinary for public houses to change their names and an event such as the race would provide as good a reason as any. Here we have the stuff of legend, and it is hardly surprising that such an entertaining story should be passed down and improved with each telling; but how true is it? Was the Grey Mare originally known by another name? Did the local Vicar really challenge one of his flock to a horse race with such provisos? And last, but by no means least, was there ever such a character as Besom Sam Higginbottom?

In a search for the truth behind this entertaining story I have consulted various sources; the most valuable, without a doubt, being Miss Lena Matthews, Besom Sam's last surviving granddaughter who is a very alert nonagenarian with a remarkable memory.

The first question is easily disposed of; the Grey Mare was built in 1811 and was called by that name well before Sam was born. If you do not believe it, then take a peep into Pigot's Directory for 1818. It is a pity to debunk such a colourful part of the story; it does not mean that the rest is a fabrication, but it certainly casts the first real doubt on its authenticity.

On the subject of the hero of the tale we are on much firmer ground, there certainly was a Sam Higginbottom. His origins are not absolutely clear as in the censuses he gives his place of birth as either New Mills, Mellor or Slack. He was probably christened at Mill Brow Independent Chapel on 30th March, 1826. He earned his living in a number of ways; as a collier; as a carrier walking between Charlesworth and the Ardern Arms near Stockport Market regularly; as a sexton; and by making and selling besoms which he hawked round on the back of his donkey. Sam made his besoms by binding ling to ash or willow handles.

He married Martha Roberts at St John's around 1851, and in 1861 the family were living in Sandy Lane, Chisworth, when Sam was employed as a coal miner. The couple are reputed to have had seventeen children. This may seem an exaggeration, but the censuses of the nineteenth century reveal eleven born between 1853 and 1872 and there are gaps between them sufficient for others who could have died in childhood. A search of St John's Register of Baptisms should soon clear up the matter. Ten of their children lived to marry and furnish Sam with forty grandchildren. Goodness knows how many folks in the district can now claim descent from Besom Sam, they must run into dozens.

Higginbottom and its variants is a very common surname in the district and there are at least two more Sam Higginbottoms buried at the Top Chapel, but they were not our man and can safely be eliminated from enquiries. The hero of our tale is buried there in a vault. As you enter the graveyard by the bottom gate, the vault lies to the left of the path, opposite the War Memorial. It is marked by a stone inscribed 'SAMUEL HIGGINBOTTOM VAULT ENTRANCE'. Sam dug the grave himself and lay in it to be quite sure it was long enough.

Samuel Higginbottom's Vault.

Charlesworth Independent Top Chapel, showing portions of Besom Sam's wall.

It is interesting that Sam should be buried at the Top Chapel after being married and his children baptised at Charlesworth Church. Perhaps his ancestors were buried at the Top Chapel which had been serving Charlesworth folk for centuries before the Church was built. Sam won the contract to build the wall around the Top Chapel graveyard; it is well worth examining as an example of the dry stone waller's craft, still being in good order well over 100 years later. This contract is recorded in the Chapel minutes and could well have been the very thing to upset the new Vicar at St John's and cause Sam to change his allegiance. Sam died on the 26th of June, 1892 and the Chapel records give the cause of death as a diseased stomach. On the day of his funeral, three days later, the cortege stretched from the Chapel doors right down Town Lane. The mourners were all on foot, villagers paying their last tribute to a man who only wanted to serve his fellow men.

Investigations reveal that Sam was far from the drunken reprobate of legend. He might not have been able to read or write, and certainly enjoyed a smoke and drink, but he had a good name throughout the district for scrupulous honesty. Delivering goods daily with his horse and cart, he was never known to be a penny out. One day when on his travels, he sat down by the watering trough at the Devil's Elbow on the turnpike road to Marple (now a lay-by due to road straightening) and found a bag near the trough and put it on his cart without checking the contents. In an age when most people in a locality were known to each other there was a good chance that he would come across the owner in the course of his travels.

A little further along the road a man came dashing along in an agitated condition. *"Th'art in a sweat"*, said Sam *"what's to do with thi?"*

The man told how he had lost his bag which Sam promptly handed over. The owner was greatly relieved and said, *"A while back I met a man who said he hoped for my sake that Besom Sam would find the bag, for then I would be sure to get it back. Did you look inside?"*

"No," said Sam, *"but I heard it chink when I dropped it in t'cart."* The bag contained all the man's money.

At Lea Head, not far from the Toll-bar at the end of Woodseats Lane, there once stood a Methodist Chapel which later became a Liberal Club. Besom Sam would stand outside and announce, *"This used to be the House of God but now it is a den of thieves,"* but that did not stop him going into such a sink of iniquity for a drink.

If you call in the Grey Mare today you will find a painting of Besom Sam and his grey mare by local artist Jim Andrew. It is not the only painting in existence of Besom Sam Higginbottom, there were at least three completed well over a hundred years ago, during his lifetime. They show a slim man very different from the stocky figure conjured up by Jim Andrew. The originals depicted Sam and his donkey with a load of besoms standing in Coombs Lane and were painted by a local cow doctor (veterinary surgeon in today's parlance) to supplement his beer funds. Sam named his donkey Palmer because it was born on the morning that the infamous murderer Doctor Palmer was hanged. This tells us a little about Sam's sense of humour. One of the paintings was destroyed during the Second World War. It had been sent away to be professionally cleaned but was damaged beyond repair during a bombing raid when it was being returned by railway. The second used to hang in the Arden Arms at Stockport; it was part of the goodwill of the house and was not to be given away or sold. Alas, it is no longer there, the present landlord has no knowledge of it and cares even less, another little bit of history lost for ever. The third painting once hung in the Commercial at Turn o't' Lane and Sam's daughter tried to buy it from the landlord. At first he refused to sell, but when he discovered who she was, and why she wanted it so badly, he let her have it for five shillings. Today it hangs in the home of Miss Lena Matthews, who has made arrangements for it to be passed on to one of Besom Sam's great great grandchildren.

Doctor William Palmer deserves a mention here; he lived in Rugeley, Staffordshire, and carved himself a niche in the halls of wickedness by a series of horrific murders. He poisoned his wife and mother-in-law and others in order to claim the insurance on their lives. He even poisoned his own illegitimate children so as to avoid paying for their upkeep. The uncovering of these crimes caused such revulsion in Rugeley that a special law, still known as the Palmer Act was rushed through Parliament which would allow the prisoner to elect for trial in London if he thought he would not get a fair hearing in his own district.

Doctor Palmer stood trial at the Old Bailey in May 1856 and was later executed in Stafford on a gallows built extra high so that the huge crowd could see the spectacle. These shocking events and the attendant publicity gave Rugeley considerable exposure in the press and brought crowds of sightsers to the town which in the short term was good for local business. Later the town wanted to forget the notoriety and eventually petitioned the government for permission to change its name. Lord Palmerston, who was the Prime Minister of the day, said, *"Certainly they can change it, why don't they name it after me?"*

The full story of Besom Sam will almost certainly never be revealed, and to date I have failed to find a shred of evidence that the horse race ever took place. Miss Matthews had certainly never heard of it before it appeared in the local paper. What certainly has emerged is a picture of a man with a sense of humour who was no saint, but who had earned the trust of his neighbours because of his honesty.

You may think it unlikely that a Vicar would indulge in a public horse race with such a result hanging on the wager. If there is a shred of truth in the story then there is only one candidate for the position of the horse racing Vicar since someone from another parish was hardly likely to be involved. The Minister at the Top Chapel, the Rev Adamson, would have been too old, and a man who did not believe in the playing of music as part of religious services was hardly likely to have indulged in wagers or horse races.

On the 26th December 1845, the Rev Goodwin Purcell was appointed to the living at Charlesworth. His earlier experiences at Charlesworth are told in a book entitled 'Stone Upon Stone'. Determined to build a church he stumped the country and managed to collect £1,500 towards the £2,700 required. The Rev Purcell's dilemma was that there were no rich gentry in Charlesworth to whom he could turn for assistance. He tells of his struggles to raise the funds and the opposition he met with. He travelled on foot, with two shirts tied on his back and an umbrella in his hand, starting early in the day so as to arrive at a convenient time to meet the local worthies who he hoped would subscribe to his fund. He had first to find a piece of land and eventually purchased one from Lord Howard for £300.

On one of his money-raising expeditions he was told not to waste his time by asking one wealthy lady for a subscription as she was so mean that she had recently disinterred a near relative in order to sell the lead from his coffin. The plumber who purchased the lead did exceedingly well from the transaction, since he cut the lead into small pieces and sold them as curios. Despite this warning, the Rev Purcell called upon the lady. She listened carefully to what he had to say and donated £5.

His description of life in Charlesworth when he arrived is probably typical of many places in the mid-nineteenth century.

'Dog and cockfights were common Sunday amusements, while the uproarious noises in public houses gave the day a sad pre-eminence in sin. Feelings of decency were outraged in many ways which it would distress my readers to describe. During the first two months after my appointment to the district I found only four church people. So completely was the place given over to Dissent and Indifferentism that at first I almost despaired of being able to gather a congregation of ten persons.'

But when Mr Purcell set himself to uproot what he termed 'the heresy of dissent', he found it a more difficult undertaking than building a Church structure. The Congregational cause at Charlesworth had been established for centuries and was not to be easily overthrown. The result was much bitterness; stones were thrown through his study window and Chapel people would spit at the Church as they passed. There were even folks in Charlesworth who would not speak to their neighbour if he attended the other place of worship.

At one time the Rev Purcell suggested that the water in Charlesworth wells was running through the bodies in the Chapel graveyard on its way down the hillside. They were 'drinking the broth of their ancestors' bones', was the way he put it. As a result the water was tested and found to be perfectly acceptable for drinking, so this attack upon the Chapel failed. Strangely there used to be a well called the Mouzy Well in the field below St John's Church. After the graveyard was opened people would no longer use the water because they feared it was contaminated.

Mr Purcell was the sort of man who, if he came to a five barred gate, would leap over it rather than bother to open it. He was to earn the name of the 'Fighting Parson', because of his willingness to tackle any person or issue. He had trained at Trinity College, Dublin, before coming to England and used to speak at public meetings denouncing the Disestablishment of the Church of Ireland, Popery, Gladstone and Bright, and anyone else who did not meet with his approval. The Rev Purcell was a man usually in the public eye and not shy about advertising his views on political and religious matters in an age when adherents of the various factions thought little of cracking each other over the head with cudgels. Whilst the story of the race is almost certainly a complete fabrication, if it had ever taken place, then the Rev Goodwin Purcell would have been the very man to have given it a go.

The true story of Besom Sam Higginbottom is quite interesting enough without flights of fancy concerning wagers on the result of a horse race for which I have failed to find a scrap of confirmation, or yarns about horses being put to bed in a local public house.

Before leaving the Higginbottoms, the following anecdotes about his wife Martha give a real insight into the hard lives of working folks of 150 years ago:

The family lived for a period at the Pistol Farm which stands on the Gun Road within the Township of Mellor. Martha would walk regularly to Glossop Market going by Coombs, Duns Clough and Chunal, carrying a basket of eggs on one arm and a baby on the other. With seventeen children, there would always be a baby! Having sold her eggs she would make the return journey, this time carrying a basket of groceries. A round trip of eight miles on some very rough tracks.

In those days the Wakes lasted for only two days and every year at that time the bedrooms and kitchen were whitewashed and new beds made. The beds consisted of hessian palliasses which were stuffed with new mown hay. These beds had to last until the next year. The reward for all the hard work was a night at the fair which came with the Wakes.

Bakewell Petty Sessions, 12.12.1874: Exposing a Child Suffering From Fever

Ellen Bye, of Dronfield, married woman, was charged with wilfully exposing a child, which was suffering from scarlet fever, in a railway carriage.

Defendant in reply to the charge said, *"I went to the station with the child, but was not aware that I was doing anything wrong."* (The defendant had a child in her arms in the court and another child sitting in the body of the court)

Doctor Knox, a witness in the case said that in all probability the child was still suffering. *"Good God,"* said the Chairman, *"Why was it brought into court then?!"*

Rough Justice

A thief was seen stealing a loaf of bread in Bakewell, apprehended and taken before a magistrate. The baker insisted that he be punished for the offence but to the surprise of the magistrate the audacious thief stated that the loaf was underweight and the baker was the one who should be punished. The magistrate ordered that the evidence be weighed and found the complaint to be justified so he sent for more loaves from the baker's shop. These all proved to be underweight so the matter ended with both the thief and the baker being punished.

The Bakewell Riots

During the Napoleonic Wars, forces of militia were raised throughout the counties of England as a counter to the threat of invasion. The miners of the High Peak were firmly of the opinion that the method of balloting for men to be recruited into the militia was unfair and this led to serious rioting in the year 1796. In time of war the miners must have been receiving a better price for their lead and earning far more than they could ever hope to get as soldiers, which would be another factor adding to their dissatisfaction. The ensuing riots in Bakewell were so uproarious that the magistrates afterwards decided to remove the holding of the sessions from Bakewell to Derby where they have stayed ever since.

The miners in the surrounding villages, being convinced that the Derbyshire Militia were raising more men and more money than other counties, agreed to march to Bakewell en masse and oppose the business of the magistrates. And so it came about that on market day, while the farmers were dining at the White Horse Inn, the waitress dashed into the room shouting, "The mob is coming, the mob." On receiving this intelligence, the farmers decided to ignore the threat and carry on dining. Soon a mob of some forty or so raw-boned men with clubs, clot-spades, miners spades and other weapons marched past the White Horse and on to the Town Hall where they made a speech signifying their intention of returning on the day of the magistrates' next meeting and putting an end to their business. Having stated their resolve they retired to the White Horse, where they borrowed a frying pan from the landlady and each paid for, and drank, a gill of ale before marching off once more. No one in the town joined the insurgents, but laughed at the spectacle, thinking them a set of hot-heads unlikely to be seen or heard of again.

They were sadly mistaken in this supposition; on the day of the Sessions, a huge mob came marching into Bakewell from Castleton, Longstone, Eyam, Baslow, and other mining villages. They stormed the Town Hall and took all the lists of men liable to serve in the militia from the officers, even being so audacious as to burst into the room where the chairman Dr Denham was seated and to proceed to search his pockets.

Once satisfied that they had possession of all the papers they made a bonfire of them outside the White Horse.

There must have been a lot more to this outrageous affair than the accounts of the time tell us. Many of the mining villages named are within easy walking distance of Bakewell, but it is a fair tramp from Castleton and one can only speculate on how such a demonstration was organised in order to gather a crowd from dispersed communities without the authorities getting wind of what was planned, especially after the earlier demonstration. It should be borne in mind that it was the practice of magistrates and the Government of the day to employ paid spies to infiltrate any group considered to be subversive.

All this took place in the days well before the establishment of county police forces, so there was no one to maintain law and order other than local parish constables, the Derbyshire Constabulary only coming into existence in 1857. The gentlemen of the town offered their assistance to the magistrates asking to be sworn in as special constables. Their offer was rejected, but before their next meeting the magistrates took the wise precaution of applying for the cavalry of the county to attend. When the mob once more assembled they were dispersed by the cavalry and six prisoners taken under military escort to Chesterfield next day. None of the prisoners came from Bakewell. With the mob safely out of the way, the magistrates were able, somewhat belatedly, to complete their business.

The gentlemen of the town provided accommodation for the cavalry during their stay in Bakewell and the costs incurred in connection with the eating, drinking and stabling of the cavalry totalled £136 10s 3d.

On the opening of the new ring of eight bells for the Church on 26th February 1797, there was a dinner at the White Horse Inn. During the evening, Mr Bossley, the Chairman, was called out and on his return announced that the Roxburgh Fencibles were coming. (A Fencible was a soldier liable only for home service). They marched in the very next day and were quartered in the town for some months where their behaviour was exemplary. Their arrival effectively put an end to the disturbances.

The White Horse Inn stood a short distance along the road to Ashford and has vanished without trace.

Hayfield 13.10.1877

The Proverb 'That it is better to dwell in the corner of the house top, than with a brawling woman in a wide house,' was aptly illustrated last week, in a house not a hundred miles from the village Church. The noise made by the termagent spouse was so great that a large crowd was attracted, who hooted and cheered the unhappy couple as they were heaping their vile epithets on one another.

Bakewell Old Town Hall, King Street, dating back to 1709.

Gargoyles on Bakewell church spire.

Free Emigration To South Australia

The Government of South Australia grants free passages to the following artisans: Carpenters, Bricklayers, Masons, Plasterers and bona fide Agricultural and Railway Labourers, not exceeding forty years of age, single or married, with not more than three children; also to single Domestic Servants. **No Miners Wanted**.

A Parson's Creed

A satirical poem said to have been found in a silver snuff-box during alterations in Bakewell Church:

> Money, oh money, thy praises I sing.
> Thou art my saviour, my God and my King.
> 'Tis for thee that I preach, for thee that I pray
> To make two collections on each Sabbath Day.
>
> I have candles and all sorts of dresses to buy,
> For I wish you to know my Church is called High;
> I don't mean the structure or steeple, or wall,
> But so high that the Lord cannot reach it at all.
>
> I have poor in my parish who need some relief.
> I preach for their poverty, pray for their grief.
> I send my box round to them morning and night
> And hope they will remember the poor widow's mite.
>
> I gather my knowledge from wisdom's great tree,
> And the whole of my trinity is L.S.D.
> Pounds, shillings and pence are all that I crave
> From my first step on earth to the brink of the grave.
>
> And when I'm laid low and my body's at rest,
> Place a box on my grave, 'tis my latest request,
> That friends may all see who come for reflection
> I can't rest in peace without a collection.
>
> Money's my creed, I'll not profit without it,
> My heaven is closed to all them that doubt it,
> For this is the essence of parsoned religion,
> Come regular to Church and be plucked like a pigeon.
>
> My pay may be hundreds or thousands a year,
> Double it, treble it, still I am here,
> With my box and my bag collecting your brass,
> I can't do as Jesus did, ride on an ass.

Th'owd Wakes

The popular idea of a Wakes Week is one where northern mill workers in cloth caps and clogs leave their home towns en masse for Blackpool, Morecambe, New Brighton, or Scarborough. Whilst this might have been true for a period after the building of the railways made cheap travel possible for many, the Wakes is a remnant of a much older tradition.

The Oxford Dictionary definition of wake is: 'The local annual festival of an English parish, observed (originally on the feast of the patron Saint of the church, but now usually on some particular Sunday and the two or three days of the week following) as an occasion for making holiday, village sports etc.'

A little investigation will usually reveal that the Wakes also coincides with the date on which the village church was consecrated or reconsecrated, which is hardly surprising since it is normal to consecrate the church on a date coinciding with the feast of its patron Saint.

More recently, the date of Wakes Weeks has been altered to suit the whims of local millowners or even to placate a public demand for a change to a week when there might be a chance of better weather. Everybody knows that it always rains at Oldham Wakes, or Stalybridge Wakes, or any other Wakes you care to mention. As a result of these changes, in some places, in addition to the official Wakes, there is also a time known as the Old Wakes.

Townships in close proximity often had different Wakes, for example in 1869 Glossop Wakes started on the 9th of September, but nearby Whitfield and Charlesworth settled for the 1st of August.

William Wood, in his 'Tales and Traditions of the High Peak,' gives the following description of these earlier customs:-

'In the Peak there is no festivity equal to the Wakes or Feast. Every village on this occasion assumes a different aspect; the inhabitants put on their best attire; all employment ceases; the cottages are adorned in rural splendour. Of the customs and practices connected with this festivity there is one which is singularly pleasing and social; that is the assembling of friends and particularly relatives from distant places at the house of their respective kinsfolk, at the Wakes. While thus assembled, every kind of recreation is brought within the sphere of innocent indulgence; and the good things of this world, carefully prepared for the occasion serve not a little in giving zest to the pleasure and pastimes of these rural merry meetings.'

These Wakes were times when old English games were indulged in and old customs renewed. Rush bearing was one such custom, and a necessary one, because in those times there were no pews for the common people and carpets were unknown. Rushes were always available and they answered well for the purpose of keeping the worshipper's feet and knees from the cold stone flags. Each yeoman was expected to furnish his share for the use of his family and labourers.

There was no better time for renewing the rush carpet than at the annual feast. At first, probably each person would convey his share by his own cart or on his back, but eventually neighbours would unite to convey the rushes. Rivalry would spring up between the people of the different hamlets, and the rushes would be stacked on the cart as neatly as possible; then decorations would gradually become general until the rush cart of 150 years ago developed.

The rushes were tied in bundles of a uniform length and circumference, the ends being cut square; they were then piled close together and formed into a pyramid, a small platform being left at the top, which was generally occupied by some local character armed with a can and string, so that he could wind up his share of ale at the ale-houses where it was customary to give the dancers an allowance. Each of the four sides had coloured or white material, carpets or calico, suspended from the top to the bottom, on which was hung the copper kettles and other articles that were intended to be given as prizes, and silver plate loaned by the gentry. The edges were decorated with ribbons and flowers. The rush cart was drawn by a team of gaily decorated horses, and the harness polished as for a horse parade. On each side were two or three men with long whips to clear a passage and keep a space for the dancers, each of the whip men vying with each other to make the loudest crack, to the delight of the boys and girls who followed them.

At the head of the procession were several men who in turns carried a garland of flowers, a work of floral art and beauty. The dancers were sixteen in number, their hats decorated with artificial flowers and ribbons borrowed from their sweethearts and friends, white shirts, the sleeves tied with bows of ribbons, knee breeches with a bow at the knees, red braid down the side of each trouser leg; in their hands they held wands of cloth, tightly rolled and decorated. The dancers were young men in the prime of life, and had previously been practising for weeks the 'Morris Dance.' The local band played the 'Freemason's Jig,' and of course there were nice young ladies with their best smiles and collecting boxes to coax the spectators to give a contribution to the expense.

The principal streets and residences were visited, stops being made at the alehouses for liquid refreshments, bandsmen and Morris dancers not generally being abstainers. Arriving at the church, the decorations were taken off and safely stored to be returned to their owners, and the rushes carried into the church and placed in position as the Churchwardens directed.

Thomas Middleton JP, of Hyde, in a paper entitled 'Rush-bearing and Morris Dancing,' gives us the following accounts:-

'In Stalybridge, the Brushes Valley supplied the bulk of the rushes, but the Stalybridge men held that the best brand of rushes could only be obtained at Fiddler's Green at the summit of the Woodhead Pass. The young men would leave home on Saturday afternoon, walk to Fiddler's Green, remain on the spot all

Old Glossop Market Cross, starting point for foot races held during the Wakes week.

Bull's Head, Old Glossop , one of at least six pubs which stood within a hundred yards of the Market cross. The bull ring is buried under the road to the left of the picture. Note the much older two storey building to the right.

night, and when daylight came, gather as many rushes as they could carry, returning with their loads on Sunday night.

(To spend all night in the open at the summit of the Woodhead Pass sounds like a recipe for death by exposure, but Thomas Middleton omits to point out that there was an inn, called the Plough and Harrow, which closed in 1851, situated at Fiddler's Green which puts an entirely different complexion on the proceedings).

Local jealousy between neighbouring villages as to the merits of their respective displays often led to serious conflicts. Whenever the rush cart and Morris dancers of Stalybridge met with those of Dukinfield or Ashton-under-Lyne, fierce battles ensued. The inhabitants of each village would attend the wakes rush-bearings of adjacent villages ready to uphold the reputation of their own celebrations with physical force.

Glossop appears to have been the scene of some of the most exciting of these combats. The trouble usually started after the trail hunt which invariably involved wagers on the dogs. The wind-up was generally a terrific fight, when the partisans of the various districts had become sufficiently inflamed with drink and carried away with the excitement of their enthusiasm and quarrels. Eyewitnesses tell us that the belligerents, sometimes a score at once, doffed their shirts, and fought with fists and feet like demons. The battles generally culminated in a melee, when stalls were overturned, and their commodities squandered pell-mell, while the disgraceful scene did not end until the length of the street had been fought over, and the participants, battered and blood-stained, were forced to give in from sheer exhaustion.'

This is clearly a scurrilous attack on the good peakland folks of Glossop by the benighted savages who live to the west. It reads more like a description of Ashton Market on a typical Saturday night. The intelligence that folks took their shirts off before setting about one another is also suspect. I clearly remember being told by a very old man who was well versed in such matters that it was unwise to take off one's jacket before fighting as there was a very good chance that someone would pinch it while you were thus engaged.

It did not require the Wakes or a trail hunt to precipitate a brawl between the inhabitants of different townships. These folks had very long memories. When the Romans worked the lead mines of the Peak, they employed both slaves and convict labour. To this day there are those who will tell you quietly that the inhabitants of the next village are the descendants of the slaves; these good folks will quickly respond by telling you that your informants are descended from the convicts. It would only require a few exchanges concerning each other's ancestry for the fists and feet to start flying.

The sports were many, and entered into with vigour as each competitor fancied his chance of winning first prize in the event for which he had entered. Of course, each hamlet backed their local fancy. The foot racing was generally a keen affair; the same courses being followed each year through the country lanes. Pigeon racing was also indulged in, and trail hunting had many patrons. Handbell ringing, quoits and bowling were among the gentler activities. Wrestling and fighting took place, the local champions generally leaving it to Wakes time to settle who was the best man. Flower and vegetable shows were held and prizes given. Each cottager had a garden and there was keen competition amongst the amateur gardeners, especially among the gooseberry growers.

At the ale-houses there was generally a musician engaged to play for dancing. During the day the church bells were ringing, the ringers from neighbouring churches trying their skill against the local ringers. After the expansion of the cotton and woollen trades, the mills stopped Monday, Tuesday and Wednesday, so there was ample time for the various games and events.

Climbing a greasy pole for a leg of mutton and catching the greasy pig took place in a field, where the bear baiting might also be held. These animals were owned by men who travelled with them from village to village. The bear was muzzled and fastened with a chain to a stake; owners of dogs paid sixpence each for the privilege of slipping their dogs at the bear, which was capable of giving the dogs some terrific blows, and if a dog got hold of his skin the bear would roll over and crush his tormentor. Owners often lost their dogs owing to the bear hugging them to death. The proceedings were occasionally enlivened by an inebriated spectator attempting to wrestle with the bear.

The bull baiting was another popular sport and in some villages the stake and ring still remain. A fee was paid as in bear baiting and the man in charge was known as the bullart. Sometimes the bull's nose was blown full of pepper in order to enrage it. The sport consisted in two or three dogs being set loose on the bull and trying to seize it by the nose and keep its head to the ground, because, if the bull attempted to toss the dog, the weight of the dog caused the bull intense pain. The dog that held the bull's head down longest won the prize or bet, but the dog was not always the winner, often tossed high in the air and killed or injured. When this happened, the dog's owner would try to catch the dog before it struck the ground. The bulls used were very wary and used to the game, but sometimes the dogs got such a grip of the bull's throat that their mouths had to be forced apart with poles. It could be a dangerous amusement, as sometimes the chain broke and the audience disappeared as fast as their legs could carry them.

The following is an extract from The Manchester Guardian of 160 years ago:

'Bull Baiting - The manly amusement of bull baiting, forms so attractive an amusement in the High Peak of Derbyshire as to be carried on under municipal patronage and it is well worthy of record that during the last week the Vicar (Rev C. Howe), Churchwardens (John Dearnally and Samuel Avison) and Constable of one of the most extensive and popular parishes in that district, Glossop, attended an auction sale for the express purpose of purchasing a bull of superior blood and

acknowledged courage, to be baited for the gratification of the inhabitants at the approaching Feast.'

The Eyam bull ring is still in existence; in 1912 it was exposed and covered with an iron plate. Later it was moved and can be seen mounted in the pavement.

Badger baiting was also popular because they could be trapped in the wild and it was thus much cheaper than bull and bear baiting, the Cheshire badger being reckoned the best. The badger was placed in a box or kennel, the front of which had an aperture sufficiently wide for a dog to enter, but not to turn round in it. The dog had to drag the badger out, and it required considerable skill and courage, for the badger can inflict a severe bite and a dog once bitten could seldom be induced to try again, though three entries were allowed.

Cock fighting was also much in demand, and regrettably is still carried on secretly in some parts of the country. Matches were held to see who had the best fighting cock with wagers placed on the result and charges being made for admission to the contest. The cocks were fitted with silver spurs and would peck and hack at each other, often slitting their crops and combs which would bleed dreadfully. Any bird which tried to escape would be seized and thrown back into the fray.

Dogs were also bred and trained specifically to fight one another. It is interesting to note that these sports of the common man have all been outlawed but sports such as fox and stag-hunting, indulged in by the well-heeled, have still managed to survive.

It was not only animals who suffered. 'Riding the Stang' was a great sport - for those who were not riding. It was secretly organised and the hapless victim would be

Eyam Bull Ring

unaware of his fate until the actual moment he or she was seized. It was a punishment publicly administered principally to adulterous women and wife beaters. The victim was collared and securely strapped to a short length of ladder, which was then hoisted with one man at each end pushing their heads between the staves and resting it on their shoulders, and the procession paraded round the village. The stang and its rider were accompanied by a crowd of men, women and boys, who provided 'rough music' by blowing whistles and beating tin cans, and the ringleader having composed a doggerel rhyme about the victim, recited this en route. This provision of rough music could be a reminder of the practice in earlier centuries of a band of musicians preceding criminals on their way to gaol. As Chaucer puts it in one of his 'Canterbury Tales,' they were 'led off with minstrelsy to gaol.' In some localities the stang consisted of a pole or a pannier slung from a pole and victims were carried off by force to a local inn and only released on payment of a sum to be spent on ale.

There were barrel rolling contests and yards of ale to be drunk. Yet another popular stunt was the pram race in which a 'baby' was rushed through the streets from pub to pub and had to consume glasses of ale at each. The pram pusher received nothing for his efforts, after all it would hardly do to be arrested on a charge of being drunk in charge of a pram.

Such rough antics were indulged in at other times besides the Wakes. At Little Hucklow the one who remained last in bed on Shrove Tuesday was called the 'bed churl' and was swept out with a broom. On this day the miner who arrived late at his work was balanced on a pole and tipped down a nearby hillock. At Abney the bed churl was forced to ride the stang to the ash midden.

These sports may be judged barbaric by today's standards but it must be borne in mind that people lived much closer to nature. Before the discovery of anaesthetics, pain just had to be suffered whether it was a tooth being pulled or a limb amputated. People who had to suffer pain would not worry overmuch about inflicting pain on an animal. Animals would be slaughtered by the local butcher with blood trickling down the street, and cottagers' fat pigs would be slaughtered on the premises. Even small children would be used to such sights. My cousin tells me of how, in the late 1920s he was one of a gang of lads employed to pull a cow with a rope up a ginnel in Old Glossop so that it could be secured to a ring in the wall, ready for slaughter. The skin and bones, etc, were afterwards taken to a factory at Spout Green in Mottram.

There were no Public Health Acts, no restrictions on keeping animals within a certain distance of human habitation, and so everyone who had the least piece of land kept pigs to fatten for the Wakes feasting. Huge jars of red cabbage and onions were put into pickle. In readiness for the event every house was whitewashed throughout and every downstairs floor stoned and sanded. Larders were filled and there was homebrewed ale in plenty. The Wakes dinner was looked forward to as one of the feasts of the year and ample justice done to it. The Wakes stalls were set up in some convenient central spot and well patronised by the young people. Occasionally a travelling theatre would come and entertain with 'blood and thunder' dramas. The various local organisations would hold processions through the streets with banners, all dressed in the regalia of their lodges of Shepherds, Oddfellows, etc.

Not everyone approved of working folks enjoying themselves as the following comments by the Rev A. Macauley show:

'But with the lower sort of people, especially in the manufacturing villages, the return of the wakes never fails to produce a week, at least, of idleness, intoxication and riot, these and other abuses, and by which the festivities are so grossly perverted from the original end of their institution, render it highly desirable to all the friends of order, of decency, and of religion, that they were totally suppressed.'

A Selection of Peakland Wakes Dates for 1878

Ashford	1st Sunday after Whit Sunday
Bugsworth & Hayfield	1st Sunday after September 19th
Bakewell	Sunday after November 5th
Baslow	1st Sunday in August
Charlesworth	1st Sunday after August 1st
Chapel	1st Sunday after September 18th
Cressbrook	Nearest Sunday to June 24th
Eyam	Last Sunday in August
Glossop	1st Sunday after September 12th
Hathersage	Sunday nearest September 11th
Tideswell	Sunday nearest June 24th
Wardlow	1st Sunday after September 11th

The Duke of Devonshire

Manchester Guardian 1.10.1825

The late Duke of Devonshire and his brother Lord George Cavendish were alike remarkable for their taciturnity, and would pass whole months together without uttering a single word. They were travelling through Europe in the same carriage, when stopping one evening in Germany they were informed, after supper, that they could only be accommodated with a chamber containing three beds, one of which was already occupied. They made no remark, but quietly proceeded to the apartment. They, however, felt some little curiosity and drawing aside the bed curtains, they took a peep at the occupant. They immediately got into bed and slept soundly.

Next morning, after they had breakfasted and paid their bill, the Duke could not refrain from saying to his brother,' "George, did you see the dead body?" "Yes." was the reply and they both got into their chaise and proceeded on their journey.

From "An Historical and Literary Tour in England and Scotland, by a foreigner: An Insight Into How The Other Half Lives":

The Duke of Devonshire had a fine table with an exquisite top made from a piece of Derbyshire Blue John and this was loaned for display to the Great Exhibition of 1851. The Duke was quite taken with the splendid table as he strolled round the exhibition, "I must get a table like that for myself," he announced.

The Life of a Gentleman

In 1804, more than 200 French prisoners of war, all officers, were held at Ashbourne. They were sworn on their parole of honour not to attempt to escape. Among them were three of Napoleon's Generals, Boyer, Pajeau, and Roussambeau, who with their retinues spent £30,000 annually in the town. According to the rules of government, the French prisoners were restricted from going more than a mile beyond the town, and then only on the public highway, and must return into the town by 9 pm when a bell was rung. If anyone was found out of their lodgings after that hour they were subject to a fine of one guinea, to be paid to the informer upon complaint before a magistrate. As a guinea was more than a week's wages for many of them, it was hardly surprising that some of the townspeople took advantage of this regulation and the volunteers, a drunken set of young fellows, would lie in wait for the officers and inform on them. This did not greatly inconvenience the French officers who were liberal with their money receiving their full pay from Napoleon and an allowance from the British Government. Being mostly men of property, they cared little for the fine which they always paid promptly. (Under such agreeable conditions of confinement there was little encouragement to escape of course)

When Lord McCartney was a prisoner in France, he received some special privileges from General Boyer. When their positions were reversed he obtained leave from the Transport Board for the General to accompany him on a tour through England, upon condition that he returned him safely back to Ashbourne, and the General accordingly accepted his invitation. While Lord McCartney and the General were enjoying their tour, Roussambeau, who was still at Ashbourne, kept up a correspondence with his friend General Boyer, and when he learned that he was returning and staying at Matlock Bath, he set out to meet him without first seeking leave to travel beyond the Ashbourne limits.

While walking alone on the Parade at Matlock Bath, he met a party of gentlemen, one of whom recognised him. The gentleman addressed him in French, and observed good naturedly that he was rather out of his limits. To this remark Roussambeau made no reply, but on his return to the inn, he made enquiries as to who the person was who had spoken to him and he learned that the gentleman was on a visit to Mr Arkwright,

Peakland Pickings

The Parade, Matlock Bath

the spinning mill owner at Cromford. General Roussambeau immediately sent him a note, with a guinea enclosed saying he supposed that was his object, being what the Ashbourne blackguards received for informing against him.

The gentleman was most indignant at this insult and immediately returned the guinea and without more ado wrote to the Transport Board in London informing them of General Roussambeau's unauthorised absence from Ashbourne, in consequence of which an order was sent down in a few days for his removal to Norman Cross Prison in Huntingdonshire, where he was held in close confinement. Shortly afterwards, being no longer restricted by parole conditions, General Roussambeau contrived to escape from detention and make his way back to France. He was eventually killed at the Battle of the Nations at Leipzig in 1813.

Not all of Napoleon's men returned to Europe at the end of hostilities as the Parish registers of St Oswald's Ashbourne testify. Some married local girls and no doubt their descendants are still to be found in the area. Their names and details also show from how wide an area the Grand Armee was recruited.

1810   13th January, Buried Felix Declamota, a Polish prisoner of war on parole of honour at Ashbourne, taken at Island of Walchern, aged 28.

1810   5th July, Buried John Lafser, a French prisoner on parole of honour at Ashbourne.

1812   27th November, Otto Ernst Heldreich, prisoner of war, married Margaret Whittaker of Ashbourne.

1816   31st May, Baptised Adolphis Leopold, son of Otto and Margaret Heldreich, Prussian.

1830   26th December, Baptised Elizabeth, daughter of Otto and Margaret Heldreich, Compton, Painter.

Disaster at Lee Valley Mill

In 1831 Lee Valley Mill, which stood by the stream which divides Chisworth from Charlesworth, was occupied by a Mr John Harrison and during his tenancy there was a serious disaster. Mr Harrison decided to construct a reservoir to supply his mill with water and, not having scientific knowledge or practical experience, built a dam which he considered would be strong enough. Some of his workers were less confident since the reservoir was close to the mill, and took the precaution of standing well clear in a safe position when Mr. Harrison let the water flow into his new reservoir on Saturday, 1st of October. The more trusting carried on in the mill.

The banks proved too weak to sustain the weight of water admitted, and gave way. The overlooker, who was stationed outside the building to watch the dam, saw the bank collapsing, and called to the workpeople. Several persons who were at work in the mill escaped, having the opportunity of getting away due to being employed on the ground floor, whilst those unfortunate enough to be on the upper storeys had no chance. The rush of water was so sudden that one man and two women had not even time to come downstairs before the building fell about them. The man's body was found in the river two miles below Charlesworth, and the bodies of the females were found near the mill.

This tragedy is typical of what were common occurrences at the time when men without the necessary experience set about constructing and modifying dams and buildings. When steam engines became more common there were many accidents caused by increasing the boiler pressure beyond safe limits in an effort to get more work out of the engine. Improvements came about because of the insurance companies rather than the efforts of the far too few factory inspectors.

John Harrison rebuilt Lee Valley Mill after the disaster and during the First World War the mill was used for making gun cotton until it was finally destroyed by fire.

The Murder of William Wood

Beside the old turnpike road from Disley to Whaley Bridge at a place called Longside there is a large stone set into the dry stone wall commemorating a shocking and senseless murder. The inscription reads:-

WILLIAM WOOD
EYAM DERBYSHIRE
HERE MURDERED
JULY 16th A.D. 1823
PREPARE TO MEET THY GOD

William Wood was a manufacturer returning from Manchester and Stockport where he had spent the previous day on business and he was carrying a considerable sum of money. The old turnpike road was a shortcut for people on foot and it is interesting that a manufacturer was prepared to walk from Stockport to Eyam rather than pay for a coach which suggests that he was in business in a very small way.

On the following Saturday the 19th, an Inquest was held at the house of Mr Sykes, the Cock Inn, Whaley Bridge, near Buxton, before John Hollins, Esq. Coroner, and a respectable jury, on the body of William Wood, of Eyam, in this county. The jury and witnesses viewed the body, which presented a horrid spectacle, the face and head being savagely mutilated, and covered with gore. On the head were ten wounds, inflicted by some blunt instrument.

The following sworn witnesses were called:- John Johnson, stonemason, and Joseph Hadfield of Disley. These local men were able to give evidence of having seen Mr Wood walking towards Whaley carrying an umbrella in his right hand and bundle or basket in the other at around seven o'clock on the previous Wednesday evening. They were also able to describe three young men who had passed along the road shortly afterwards. Two were wearing dark coloured coats and were of average size while the other was taller and wearing a light coloured jacket and trousers of a coarse material. All three appeared to be around 18 or 19 years of age. They were all going towards the place where the deceased was found.

Edmund Pott of Kettleshulme and John Mellor were returning from Stockport with a cart and horses at around eight o'clock when they came upon Mr Wood's body lying by the lower side of the road, quite dead, but still warm, with blood still flowing from the head. Several stones covered with blood lay on the road behind his head. Pott and Mellor lifted the body onto the cart and carried it to the Cock Inn in Whaley, with blood still running from the body. The stones were produced at the inquest; all very bloody, with hair still sticking to them; and one had the appearance of bloody finger marks at one end.

Thomas Etchells of Whaley, described how at about half past seven, or twenty minutes before eight, he was coming very slowly along the old road from Whaley to Disley, when he saw three men running along the road towards Whaley. When they came within about forty yards of him, they ceased running, and walked, and one of them asked him, *"How far is it to Chapel-en-le-Frith?"*

He replied *"Four miles."*

As soon as they passed him, they ran again, and continued to run till he ceased to look after them. He was able to give descriptions matching those of earlier witnesses. Also, the taller man, on his left arm, between the shoulder and the elbow, had a mark four or five inches long, the colour of blood. The place where he first saw these men, was about half a mile from the place where the deceased was found; and they were running in a direction away from that place.

John Johnson, wheelwright, of Whaley, and William Beard, labourer, of Disley, on the Wednesday evening were standing beside the Smithy at Whaley, opposite the end of the old road from Disley, when they saw three men running down that road towards them and formed the impression they were running a race. They ran about a quarter of a mile, and then stopped when they got near the Whaley Toll Gate. They went along the road towards Buxton. Two of the men were about 5 feet 7 or 8 inches high, with dark coloured coats which they took to be blue. The other man was about two or three inches taller, had on a light coloured jacket and trousers of the same colour, with a white apron round his waist. He was thin. They all appeared about twenty years of age.

Henry Scott, the toll-bar keeper at Whaley, spotted three young men after they had passed a few yards through the bar. They were walking quickly along the road towards Buxton. One had a jacket and trousers on, both light coloured, and he was without stockings. On the leg of his trousers, towards the bottom he saw blood, as well as upon his leg below the trousers.

William Wright, of Disley, surgeon, described how he had examined the body of the deceased, and found ten wounds upon the head, and forehead. They had been made by some blunt instrument. The blow on the back of the head had fractured the skull in three directions; the one an inch and a half long, and the others rather less; part of the skull was forced into the brain. This wound was calculated to produce instant death. Any of the stones produced could have inflicted such wounds as he had found upon the deceased.

No other evidence appearing to identify the murderers, the jury returned a verdict of Wilful Murder, against some person or persons unknown. None of the money which Mr Wood had been carrying was found on his body.

The murderers were not to escape from justice so easily. The following account in the Macclesfield Courier of July 19th follows their further exploits:

On Thursday morning, three young men, two rather shabbily dressed, and the third in a new fustian jacket and trousers came into this town and went to the Golden Lion public house.

Their visit was remembered by the landlady, Mrs Ellen Broadhurst, because the youngest one left and shortly afterwards returned with a parcel containing shoes and stockings, which the men changed into. The shoes and stockings were bought from Mr William Wainwright, in Chestergate. The younger of the three then proceeded to Mr Thomas Burgess's, in the same street, and purchased three complete suits of clothes, and then returned to his companions, who stated that they were related to Mr David Browne, and wished to change their clothes before they saw him. Having done so, they had some beef steaks, and left the house, one of them leaving his old clothes behind him. The youngest of the three then went into Chestergate, and told Mr Wainwright he wanted to give their old clothes away to some poor person. Mr Wainwright told he could do no better than give them to an orphan boy who stood at the shop door. Before leaving Macclesfield for Manchester on the Telegraph coach they purchased watches from John Longstaff, an apprentice watchmaker. All these people were later able to act as witnesses at the Chester Assizes.

Shortly afterwards, intelligence of the murder having reached Macclesfield, a suspicion arose that these three fellows had been concerned in the deed, and upon examining their old clothes, they were found much stained with blood. Mr Frost the constable, immediately proceeded to Manchester by the Mail coach:

We have seen the clothes of these men, they were much smeared with dirt, evidently from a lime road to conceal the blood on them, which in many places is very visible in the inside, and we have not the smallest doubt that the owners of them are the perpetrators of the bloody deed.

In the Manchester Mercury of July 22nd further details appeared which shows how news spread, even when newspapers only came out weekly:

We have to state, that on Thursday afternoon, about six o'clock, the three fellows against whom there is so strong a presumption of their having perpetrated the horrid deed, proceeded to the Greyhounds public house, in Oak Street, in this town, and called for some liquor. The landlord observing that the same persons had been at his house the day before, and presenting a very different appearance, being clothed from head to foot with altogether new clothes, and having plenty of money in their pockets, a suspicion was awakened in his mind that the men had committed some robbery, and he immediately dispatched his son to the Police-office, from whence, after communicating the intelligence, two officers accompanied him to the house, but unfortunately before they got there two of them had left; the third was, however, luckily taken

Murder stone beside the old turnpike road near Disley.

into custody, who, having first given information on the subject, was conveyed to the New Bailey prison. Diligent search was made in all directions during the night in quest of the other two, but without success. On Friday morning, they were seen drinking with some women at the Coach and Horses public house in Saint George's Road, and the landlord being struck with their appearance, sent to the Police-office, where officers were immediately forwarded, but before they reached the house they were suffered to leave, and were observed to proceed rather hastily over the fields which lead into Oldham Road, since which time we are sorry to learn no trace whatever has been discovered of them.

Shortly afterwards, the Manchester Mercury was to carry the following headline:

SELF DESTRUCTION OF ONE OF THE MURDERERS:
Charles Taylor, the person apprehended at the Greyhounds public house, was discovered about one o'clock on Friday afternoon, by Mr Evans, the turnkey, at the New Bailey, suspended on the stove pipe, which crosses the room where he was confined. The wretched murderer, it appears, had tied his stockings together, and with the assistance of his garters, was enabled to make them sufficient for the fatal purpose. He was not quite dead when found, but had so far effected his fatal purpose, that he had not been able to speak since, and he died on Sunday morning, about three o'clock. He was a native of Salford, and has lived for some time in Oldfield Road, is 17 years of age, and has been twice convicted of felony. The other characters are equally young and have but a short time since left the New Bailey; they are all so well known that they cannot with any degree of probability remain long at liberty.

Taylor had made a full confession and named his accomplices as Platt and Dale. According to his version of events it was Platt who struck Mr Wood a violent blow with a stone and knocked him down.

The Manchester Guardian of 26th July, 1823 had some scathing comments for the local authorities and their efforts to bring the culprits to justice:
We understand that a very culpable negligence has been displayed by the constables of the township where the murder was committed. They have not offered any reward for the apprehension of the murderers, nor (as we are informed) taken any steps to find them out. All that has been hitherto done for this purpose, has we believe been at the expense of G. W. Newton Esq., a neighbouring magistrate and by the constables of Manchester.

A reward of 20 guineas each for the conviction of Dale and Platt was offered. Joseph Dale was apprehended on August 9th in Liverpool where he had fled. At his trial at Chester, at the end of August, Mr Josiah Cheetham, a manufacturer of Stockport, told how he had some transactions with Mr Wood on Wednesday 16th of July and had paid him £48 and some shillings. He had made a note of the dates and numbers of several of the £5 notes.

Dale told the court that the three young men had met William Wood by chance and he had invited them into a nearby inn for a drink where they learned of the sum of money he was carrying. Dale denied having any part in the murder and stated that he had gone ahead to wait at an inn for the other two. He was unable to say where this inn was or produce any landlord to uphold his statement. When confronted with the fact that one of the Bank of England notes which Mr Wood had received in Stockport had been traced to him he admitted stealing part of the money. Dale had not previously been in any trouble with the police and three witnesses were able to speak well of his character. Nevertheless he was found guilty by association and sentenced to death by hanging.

On 9th September a young man answering closely to the description of the wanted man Platt (or Pratt) was taken to Stockport prison by Mr Lomas, the constable of Disley. The man succeeded in convincing the magistrate that he was not Platt and he was discharged.

Joseph Dale was executed at Chester City Gaol on Wednesday 21st of April, 1824. The following is the account from the Manchester Guardian of 24th April 1824: Wednesday morning at 5 o'clock. Arrived at the city gaol. The morning was spent in devotional exercises with the Rev. Keeling, in which Dale gave him well grounded assurances of his hope in death, and expressed his surprise that death could be met with so much happiness as he then felt in its contemplation. As the time for the execution began to approach, he expressed an anxiety almost amounting to impatience, for the arrival of the officers; and as soon as they arrived he begged to be immediately led out to the place of execution, which request was complied with. The execution was therefore completed before the appointed hour, but there was still a fair crowd in attendance.

Thus terminated the short career of this originally amiable young man. Without former criminal dispositions or habits, through a brief and casual association with abandoned persons, he has been brought to end his days upon the gallows, when he had scarcely completed his 18th year.

William Wood was only thirty and left a widow and three children. Platt was never caught.

The Menace of the Manchester Man

Folks are always telling me that there aren't any of the old characters about anymore; on the contrary I seem to meet them everywhere I go. Only the other morning I popped into a graveyard to do a spot of genealogical research when I came across a chap preparing his breakfast on a gravestone. My first impression was that he was employed in tidying the place, but it transpired that he had spent the night there, sleeping under a bush in a plastic bag. He told me that as he travelled around the country he always made a point of sleeping in graveyards as this guaranteed he would not be disturbed in the night. I could follow his reasoning, it must be an example of this lateral thinking which is all the rage.

Perhaps I should write a book about a few of them, but for the moment I will settle for a true story about a farmer I know; the only item altered is his name as I don't want him to set about me the next time I walk by his place.

It was a balmy Friday evening in late spring and blackbirds and thrushes were in full song as I made my way along the well trodden footpath towards Fred Bennett's farm. It was an evening which might be expected to bring out the best and most generous traits in anyone. The first indication that anything out of the ordinary was in the offing to mar the golden moment, was the sight of a large banner stretched across the path between two trees. Perhaps Fred was planning to hold a gymkhana in one of his fields that weekend; it seemed the most likely explanation since his daughter spent every spare minute riding.

On drawing closer the words PRIVATE NO ROAD could be made out clearly, and there, standing foursquare across the path was the redoubtable Fred Bennett in person. Fred was almost as broad as he was tall and was armed with a shotgun under his arm and a pair of binoculars around his neck. Something must be seriously wrong for Fred to decide to block a well used public footpath and stand there ready to repel all comers.

"What's to do Fred, surely this is a public footpath?"

"Oh, it is, you can go along it alright, but I'll be damned if any of that lot will get past me."

"What's the matter then Fred? Who on earth are you talking about?"

"It's that blasted Manchester Man who is to blame for writing these damn fool articles in the evening paper. Walks around Manchester."

"I still don't see any connection with him and your blocking up the path, Fred."

"Well I'll tell you. This week he has described a walk right through my farm and it's not coming off. That Manchester Man should come along with the clowns that read his articles and put right all the damage they do. The man's a blithering idiot."

"Surely you don't begrudge those poor folk from Manchester a spot of fresh air?" said I, knowing it would only add to Fred's fury.

Fred's face started to redden at the very thought of armies of Mancunians marching across his fields and he glowered fiercely around him.

"I wouldn't mind so much if there were just one or two of them but last time there was half of Manchester tramping through the place. I'd like to get hold of that Manchester Man and wring his flaming neck. You can take it from me none of them will get past me, right of way or not."

At that moment Fred decided to sweep the scene with his binoculars and soon spotted some youths dismantling one of his dry stone walls about 300 yards away.

"There's some of 'em at it this very minute," shouted Fred, letting fly with his shotgun in the direction of the vandals. The range was too great to do any damage but

they took to their heels as shot whistled around them. As I continued on my way Fred was in full pursuit his sturdy legs going like pistons.

That Manchester Man could have had no idea of the troubles he had set in motion in a quiet upland valley.

The Lamp of Saint Helen

Anthony Babington was born at Dethick, near Matlock, in October 1561. He is remembered as a leader of the Babington Plot to assassinate Elizabeth I and to install her prisoner, the Roman Catholic Mary Stuart, Queen of Scots, on the English Throne. The son of Henry Babington, he inherited his father's considerable estates at the age of 10. His mother and guardians adhered to the old faith and raised him secretly as a Roman Catholic. In his youth he served at Sheffield as page to the Earl of Shrewsbury who was charged with holding Mary Stuart prisoner. In 1580 he went to London to attend the court of Elizabeth I where he joined the secret society protecting and concealing the Jesuit missionaries Campion and Parsons, and in 1582, after the execution of Edmund Campion, he withdrew to Derbyshire before going abroad. In Paris, he associated with Mary's supporters who were planning her release with Spanish help. On his return he was entrusted with letters for her, and in May 1586 he was joined by the priest John Ballard in what became known as the Babington Plot.

The conspiracy was intended to destroy the government and included Roman Catholics in many parts of the country. Phillip II of Spain had promised assistance with an expedition after the Queen was assassinated. Ballard wrote to Mary explaining his plans, but his letters and her reply were intercepted by Walsingham's spies. On August 4th, Ballard was arrested and betrayed his comrades under torture. Babington, meanwhile, had applied for a passport abroad, ostensibly for the purpose of spying upon the refugees, but in reality to organise the foreign expedition and save his own life. Because the passport was delayed, he offered to reveal to Walsingham a dangerous conspiracy, but the latter, knowing what was afoot, sent no reply and gave instructions for the the ports to be closed.

Babington, thoroughly alarmed, fled to St John's Wood and after disguising himself managed to reach Harrow where he was sheltered by a Catholic convert. But at the end of August he was captured and imprisoned in the Tower of London. On September 13th and 14th he was tried with Ballard and five others by a special commission; he confessed, but strove to place the blame on Ballard. All were condemned to death for high treason. On September 19th he wrote to Elizabeth praying for mercy and the same day offered £1000 to procure his pardon:

"Anthony Babington. Prisoner in the Tower of London to her Queen's Majesty. Most gracious sovereign, if either bitter tears, a pensive contrite heart or any dutiful suit of the wretched sinner might work any pity in your Royal breast, I would wring out my drained eyes as much blood as in bemoaning my dreary Tragedy should lamentably

bewail my faults and somewhat no doubt move you to compassion - but since there is no proportion between the quality of my crime and my humane commiseration shew sweet Queen, some miracle on a wretch that lieth prostrate in your prison most grievously bewailing his offence - and imploring such comfort at your anointed hand as my poor wife's misfortune doth beg, my child's innocence doth crave, my guiltless family doth least deserve - so shall your divine mercy make your glory shine as far above all princes as my most horrible practices are most detestable amongst your baser subjects whom lovingly and happily to govern. I humbly beseech the Merciful Master himself to grant for his sweet son's sake Jesus Christ your Majesty's most unfortunate (because most disloyal) subject."

His letter was all to no avail; the next day he was executed at Lincoln's Inn Fields with great barbarity, so as to 'protract the extremitie of payne.'

On the discovery of the plot, church bells were rung throughout the land and there were bonfires and dancing in the streets in celebration because of the Queen's delivery from danger, the Queen's safety being identified by the English people with the security of the nation from foreign invasion.

These machinations of Babington and his fellow plotters were to have far reaching and unexpected consequences for an old landed family and their tenants living in a quiet Derbyshire village. In the early years of the sixteenth century, in the village of Eyam, there lived a gentleman of wealth by the name of Humphrey Stafford, the last male heir of the Staffords. The family had inherited extensive possessions in and around Eyam, from the time of King Henry III in 1252, which possessions were granted to the first of the Staffords in Eyam by that King on certain specific conditions.

Stafford Hall, their residence, stood on the north-west edge of the village. Erected in the reign of Henry VI it was a spacious building whose rooms were all floored with brightly polished black oak, and with narrow windows which combined to give the whole a sombre appearance.

Humphrey was a widower with five beautiful daughters; the eldest, Margaret (whose name has been remembered as Madame Stafford), Alice, Gertrude, Ann and Katherine, all approaching womanhood. Besides these daughters, there were two sons, Humphrey and Roland, who, sadly for their father, died in their youth. The mother, some time after giving birth to her youngest child, suffered from a severe but brief illness and was hurried to her grave. With the death of his beloved partner, Humphrey saw his cherished hope of having a male heir almost certainly never to be realised.

His aged father when lying on his death bed had given Humphrey a strict injunction. *"Humphrey, my son, listen carefully to my words before I die. I have not long for this world, but next to eternal happiness, my most fervent wish is that you will perpetuate my name and race by the fruit of your loins. Never forget to tend the lamp of Saint Helen, and take care that the name of Stafford goes down to posterity as I bequeath it to you; unstained by uncharitable ambition, tyranny or avarice."*

A short distance from Stafford Hall was the village church, an ancient, but very small building. In those days it had only a very small tower at the west end which was adorned with gargoyles. This tower contained only one small bell, which regularly tolled to call the ancient forefathers of the village to mass. In their attendance at church, Humphrey Stafford and his daughters were as faithful as the sabbath. There, in a pew abutting the north aisle, they praised God in common with the most impoverished villagers, their pew only distinguished from others by being larger.

It was the peculiar tenure by which the Staffords of Eyam held their land, that not only caused them to reside permanently at Eyam, but also to be unremitting in their attendance in Church. The tenure stated that the Staffords shall hold such lands on the express condition, *"Of keeping a lamp perpetually burning on the altar of Saint Helen, in the parish Church of Eyam."* And another item stated *"That the lamp shall be superintended by the actual male possessor, or in default of male issue, by female issue during her life on condition of her utterly abstaining from entering into a married state or marriage contract. The lands were to pass from the family at her death or marriage."*

Humphrey never married again because he never met another woman who could measure up in his estimation to the perfection of his dear dead wife, and his high principles prevented him from marrying merely for the purpose of procuring a male heir. With the passage of the years he was slowly forced to face the prospect of the Hall and lands passing for ever from the Stafford line. The reputed wealth of the Staffords brought many competitors for the hands and hearts of his daughters. Eventually they all married except Margaret who refused every solicitation for her hand. Too well she knew the cause of her good father's dejection of spirit; the certainty of their lands passing into the possession of others. Hence as her two brothers were dead and her sisters married she had formed an unshakeable resolution never to marry, but to continue the possessions of her forefathers by superintending the lamp of Saint Helen until her death.

Humphrey was frequently visited by the Rector of the village, the Rev Robert Talbot, a relation of the Earl of Shrewsbury. The two would converse for hours several times weekly. One evening at sunset, Rev Talbot had been seen to make his way to Stafford Hall with more than usual speed, and on arrival, he was ushered into the room where Stafford sat alone, buried in contemplation.

"Well Mr Stafford," said Rev Talbot, *"intelligence has just reached me that the unfortunate Mary, Scotland's Queen, has just arrived at Chatsworth, where it is intended she will stay for a few months at least. It is a long, long time since our locality was honoured by the presence of royalty."*

"Alas," replied Stafford, *"I fear that this unhappy woman is doomed to fall a sacrifice to uncontrollable circumstances; that ultimately the machinations of her enemies will be satisfied with nothing less than her life."*

"Let us hope not," replied Talbot, *"most assuredly our virgin Queen would never leave such an ineffaceable blot on the annals of her reign. What will be the judgment of*

posterity should your fears on that head be realised?"

Just as Talbot was finishing his reply, Miss Stafford entered the room and said, *"I suppose, Mr Talbot, the circumstance of Chatsworth being now the temporary residence of captive royalty, will induce numbers to congregate daily in the park with a view to having even a brief glance at misfortune's favourite."*

"Undoubtedly, you are right." replied Rev. Talbot.

"I presume papa has informed you that we have just prior to your visit, received an invitation from my Lord Shrewsbury, to pay him a visit while at Chatsworth with his royal captive; and that we have positively arranged to set out, early tomorrow."

On the morning of the following day, Stafford and his daughter rose early to make their way to Chatsworth. Mounted on swift horses, they soon covered the few miles to the Palace of the Peak where Mary was staying effectively under arrest in the care of the Earl of Shrewsbury. They were most cordially greeted by the noble Earl, to whom Stafford was related by blood. Stafford was also the Earl's representative as Lord of the Manor of Eyam, in which the Earl had a just guardian of his many interests.

A few hours after their arrival at Chatsworth Stafford and his daughter had an opportunity of seeing, from a distance, the royal captive. She was, with a few attendants, walking in the garden, where she might be seen to advantage by the Staffords from the room in which they had been placed for that special purpose. Margaret was saddened to see Mary confined in this way and fervently wished to have an interview with her before leaving Chatsworth, but she knew it would never be allowed.

Stafford and the noble Earl had a protracted private conversation, partly on the captivity of Mary, but more in particular on matters connected with the affairs of Stafford himself. The Earl had cause for concern; at that time the High Peak was still a stronghold of the Old Religion and there was the ever present risk of an attempt to rescue Mary, and if this was not sufficient, he was involved in a lengthy dispute with some of his tenants over the conditions of their new leases. With Walsingham's network of spies at work throughout the land, he had no wish for anything to occur which might call his loyalty into question, and at the same time he did not wish any harm to befall Mary while in his custody.

"I shall use every possible effort to hand over the royal prisoner now in my keeping into the charge of some other loyal person, as I have for some time apprehended a fast approaching event, which I contemplate with some degree of horror; but be assured that the object which I shall endeavour to attain, will be a work of vigilance, and will be attended with some degree of danger or disapprobation, unless circumspection be used unsparingly. And as respects the other topic of our conversation, let me positively assure you, that in case I should survive you, my dear kinsman and friend, I will use my utmost endeavours to avert the likely consequence which you naturally expect to result from the extinguishment of the lamp of Saint Helen. On me, or my successor, as Lord of the Manor of Eyam, much will depend on

subscribing the signature of the lineal representative of the first holder of the Manor of Eyam, connected with which originally was the Lamp of St Helen."

Stafford thanked the Earl kindly. It was an hour before sunset when the Staffords left Chatsworth. On reaching the dell which leads to Eyam, as they rode up the steep narrow path Margaret said, *"Oh, father I forgot this morning to write the letter which you wished me to write for you to your young friend on the continent; Mr Babington."*

"Well, my dear, it is of no great matter this day, for his friend does not leave to join him until six days hence, and besides you can give him some account of the Scottish Queen; your opinion of her person, her captivity, and its probable consequence."

One beautiful evening in 1585, soon after Stafford's visit to Chatsworth, his daughter walked out to enjoy the delights of the dell. After a little time had elapsed she was seized by a tremor as she had a dreadful premonition of some happening concerning her father at Stafford Hall. Margaret rushed back to the Hall in alarm and on reaching the gate of her home she was greeted by the frantic cries of the servants.

"He's dead, the master, our good master." Her father had been found dead in his chair while his daughter had been taking her walk.

The day arrived for the interment of the last male of the Staffords. On the top of the coffin lid the initials H.S. only were inscribed with brass nails. The coffin was born by six strong villagers and the streets were filled with men, women and little children. On arriving at the church yard, there was one manifest expression of grief; the corpse was carried once round the Saxon cross, a custom which had been observed from time immemorial, and then into the church. The Lamp of St Helen was burning on the altar of stone, and the Rev Talbot, the priest and friend of Stafford, officiated at the burial which must have been a particularly sorrowful occasion for him.

About two years after the death of Stafford, a large party of villagers were assembled at the Shrewsbury Arms which stood at the east end of a pool in the centre of the village. The sign board contained on each side a rudely painted large talbot (dog), the martial crest of the arms of the Earls of Shrewsbury. The occasion was the wakes, then held about the middle of August. It was Wake Monday, the principal day of the week's festivity, and mine host, Mr Decket, was employed in attending to his customers.

Whilst the good folks of Eyam were thus happily engaged, a stranger was riding swiftly through Middleton Dale, a sword at his side, and a letter of desperate urgency concealed about his person. Sometime towards evening, this tall young man came galloping up to the Shrewsbury Arms. leapt from his horse, and on entering the room asked in a rather agitated manner to speak with Mr Decket. After a few minutes guarded conversation at the door, Decket and the stranger proceeded to Stafford Hall at a speed that surprised everyone they met. Miss Stafford was just leaving the Hall to perform her daily task of attending to the lamp of Saint Helen when the stranger walked up to her and unfolding a paper, bid her read it with the greatest dispatch, as a few minutes delay might be attended with the most serious consequences. Filled with surprise Miss

Eyam Church.

Eyam Cross.

Stafford glanced over the contents of the paper and then exclaimed, *"Where shall I fly?"*

"Into some place of concealment immediately," said the stranger.

"My good man," he said to Deckett, *"take her away into some wood or secret cavern this moment, or the next she may be arrested for high treason. Make haste so that even your servants have no notion as to your whereabouts, then they cannot betray you by some chance remark."*

Decket hastened away with Margaret with the intention of hiding her in the Salt Pan, a deep maze-like chasm in a secluded rock near Eyam. Once there he took her to the most secret part of the place where it would be almost impossible to discover her. The young stranger meanwhile made his way back to the South by a circuitous route having no wish to fall foul of the Queen's agents whom he knew to be close on his heels.

Before leaving Miss Stafford, Decket had learned from her the particulars of the mysterious affair. On the night of her visit to Chatsworth she had written a long letter to Anthony Babington, then staying in Paris, in which she had commented on the personal attractions and the unjust imprisonment of Mary, Queen of Scots. She had written at great length on the wickedness of Mary's enemies and had expressed a desire that the Queen might be liberated and again ascend the throne of her ancestors. To this letter she had appended the name of her father as well as her own. The letter reached Babington just when he was being inveigled into the conspiracy against the life of Queen Elizabeth on behalf of the Scottish Queen and the Catholic Religion. The contents of the letter accorded well with the cause in which Babington was then blindly engaged, and he in a moment of foolishness sent the letter to Mary, with the intention of giving her the impression that she had friends of birth and quality in England. The letter was found among the private papers seized in the possession of Mary at Chertsey. It was inspected by Walsingham, who laid it before Elizabeth, and Miss Stafford and her father were ordered to be arrested without delay.

The day before Babington's apprehension at Harrow, he had written a letter to Miss Stafford, and with a purse of gold induced a friend, our stranger, to carry it to her at Eyam with all speed.

The Earl of Shrewsbury's wish to be relieved of the burden of guarding Mary was not to be granted. After holding Mary at various residences belonging to him at Sheffield, Hardwick Hall, Wingfield Hall and Buxton, on February 7th 1587, together with the Earl of Kent, he had the disagreeable duty of serving her with her death warrant. She was executed the day following.

Scarce an hour had elapsed from the time of Decket leaving Miss Stafford concealed in the Salt Pan, than four armed men arrived at his door on horses. They ordered their horses stabled and desired to be shown to Stafford Hall with all speed. Arriving at the hall they hammered on the great oak door crying, *"Open up, we are about the Queen's business."* When the startled servants opened the door, the Queen's officers demanded to know where Humphrey Stafford and his daughter were. They were speedily informed that Humphrey had been dead for some time and that Miss Stafford had shortly before left to tend the lamp at the village church. Without another word they rushed from room to room, tearing down draperies and hacking at panels. When a search of the church also failed to reveal any trace of Margaret, their rage increased to madness. They soon ascertained that Humphrey Stafford was indeed dead, but they threatened the domestics with instant death if they did not disclose to them where Miss Stafford was secreted, but all to no avail. Hour after hour passed, but the object of their search could not be found. Every room about the hall was searched and the following day all the houses in the village; Miss Stafford had disappeared.

Decket, true to his appointment, returned to Miss Stafford's shelter and under cover of darkness conveyed her to a cottage well away from any other habitation. The cottage was on Gother Edge, two miles to the north of Eyam where she remained while Stafford Hall was inhabited by the Queen's officers as a base for their operations. For many years this unhappy woman was hidden among the hills north of Eyam, in the woods and lonely defiles by day in every sort of weather, in solitary cottages at night. Decket and a few others were her guardians, always apprising her of the route her pursuers took. Still, she was numberless times in imminent danger; had hairbreadth escapes, often seeing them a short distance from her place of concealment. During these years of suffering however, she ventured many times into the village for the purpose of attending the Lamp of Saint Helen, always at dead of night when she had previously ascertained that her pursuers were absent from the place.

It was not until the death of Queen Elizabeth sixteen years later that Miss Stafford returned to the mansion of her fathers, wholly free from the fear of falling into the hands of those whom the Queen had deputed to arrest her at all peril. The villagers were intoxicated with joy as she was welcomed home.

The particulars of the sufferings of Miss Stafford, and the cause, were soon made known to King James by the successor of that Earl of Shrewsbury whom Miss Stafford and her father had visited when the Scottish Queen was at Chatsworth. The Monarch expressed much sympathy for Miss Stafford and anxiously enquired in what way she would wish to be recompensed for her long and severe trails. Then it was she saw the opportunity of obtaining what had so often engrossed her father's mind; she humbly requested the annulment of the tenure by which her forefathers held their lands at Eyam. This the monarch ordered to be done immediately; the burning of the Lamp of Saint Helen to be abolished, and the lands of the Staffords to be inherited, in fee simple, by the co-heiresses of Humphrey Stafford and their heirs for ever. The inheritance passed to the eldest of Humphrey's other daughters, Ann, who had married Francis Bradshaw, of the family of the notorious Judge Bradshaw. The Bradshaws deserted Eyam at the time of the plague and never returned.

When Miss Stafford had attained this object, she resolved to spend the rest of her days amid the consolations of religion. Besides numerous acts of charity to the villagers, she ordered the small tower of the church to be taken down, and the present one to be erected for the reception of bells. For the simple villagers, this one act, the erection of the new tower and the four bells, was deemed to be one of the greatest events 'in the womb of time.'

She was interred besides her father near the northern aisle of the church. The Lamp of Saint Helen and the ornamented stone on which it had stood on the altar for centuries were placed by her dying request at the foot of her coffin. The stone however, which contains an indented runic scroll, was taken up some years ago and may now be seen placed in the interior side of the wall, beneath the window in the eastern end of the northern aisle and contiguous to the confessional of pre-protestant times. A bronze lamp reputed to be the original lamp of Saint Helen was stolen from the church in 1984.

Note how the doings of the high and mighty impinge on the humblest in the land. The schemes of Walsingham and Babington rebounding on the honest Decket, and simple husbandmen hiding Margaret in their remote cottages. But despite all their exertions, sometimes the best laid plans are set at nought.

The Parish Church of Eyam is dedicated to Saint Lawrence, and was formerly dedicated to Saint Helen. Doubts have been cast on the veracity of this tale; it has even been suggested that William Wood invented an extra daughter for Sir Humphrey, but certainly much of it fits in well with historical fact. If William Wood added a few romantic details from his own imagination, what of it? Far better that such a fine story be preserved than lost due to too zealous a search for historical accuracy.

The Duke of Norfolk

From time to time, people with the surname Howard who are delving into their ancestry, get it into their heads that they are descended from some branch of the Howards, in the same manner that certain members of the aristocracy can claim descent from Charles II. The official answer to such flights of fancy is that there is no record of such offspring. However, if the following anecdotes are true, then these aspirants to nobility might just be on to something.

In his Reminiscences, published in 1828, Henry Angelo provided an exhaustive catalogue of the society figures of his day, among them the Duke of Norfolk:

The Duke, long addicted to self-indulgence, had an extensive and increasing list of annuities to pay to women of various grades as the wages of their shame. It was said that these were paid quarterly, at a certain banker's, the cheques being drawn payable on a certain day, to all the parties. Such frail pensioners were not likely to postpone their receipts, and aware of this, the Duke used to sit in a back parlour, to have a peep at his old acquaintances, the name of whom, as each applied, he knew as a clerk was appointed to bring the cheque as presented for the Duke's inspection. There he would make his comments to a confidential person, at his elbow.

Of one he would say, *"I'faith, she looks as young as twenty years ago,"* of another, *"What a dowdy!"* and of another, *"What an old hag!"* Occasionally, however, a feeling of compunction, or perhaps of caprice, would seize him, when he would desire the party to step in, and there, after inquiring of their welfare, strange to say, he would sometimes entertain them with a gratuitous lecture on morality.

It was not only the former mistresses who were numerous. It is recorded that once when driving through the village of Greystoke in Cumberland with his steward, he saw hordes of children waving at them from both sides of the road.

"Whose are all those children?" he asked.

The steward answered, *"Some are mine, Your Grace, and some are yours."*

Now here we have a fine example of the nuances of the English class system. It is quite in order for dukes and princes to indulge in such extra-curricular activities; indeed, we would be disappointed if they failed to do so. As for the rest of us, such behaviour is totally unacceptable. What of the Duke's Steward, you ask? What indeed? Clearly he was getting ideas above his station.

More recently, the current Duke of Norfolk paid a visit to Glossop in connection with the Royal British Legion Service of Remembrance. After the service he got into conversation with a local official and the following exchange of niceties took place.

*"Well K*****r, how are things in Glossop these days?"*

"Very well on the whole your Grace, but one thing gives me cause for concern." said the official knuckling his forehead as he did so.

"I'm sorry to hear that. Whatever is it that bothers you?"

"I am concerned about Phillip Howard Road which as your Grace is well aware, was built and named as a memorial to a member of your family who fell in the First War. If your Grace will take the trouble to take a closer look he will discover that Phillip is spelt with one l at one end of the road and with two l's at the other."

"Goodness gracious, I will see that something is done about it straight away."

The Glossop Council got around this little difficulty with ease. They just removed the sign at the bottom of the road.

Glossop: 14.11.1874

Sauce For Goose and Gander. Joseph Rhodes and Charles Heaton were separately charged with being drunk and riotous in Station Road, and both pleaded guilty. It seems they were found fighting by PCs Gibbs and Smith. Rhodes complained that they charged 1 shilling for keeping him all night in the lock-up and fourpence for breakfast.

"That is as good as staying at an hotel." said the Clerk of the Court.

The pair were fined five shillings and costs each.

Murder in the Winnats

At the beginning of his graphic version of this shocking tale, William Wood of Eyam (1804-1865), makes the following comment:

"The story of the Winnats murder is full of circumstances of an extraordinary character; love on the part of the victims; and the most striking instance on record of Divine judgment."

At Peak Forest in the High Peak, a Chapel was erected in 1657, by Christina, Countess of Devonshire, an ardent Royalist, dedicated to 'Charles, King and Martyr.' This chapel was under no parochial obligations and was not subject to any episcopal authority. As a result, the minister possessed many privileges, and was himself 'Judge in Spiritualities in the Peculiar Court of Peak Forest.' He was his own surrogate, (deputy of Bishop or his chancellor for granting licences without banns), and could grant marriage licences without any fear of consequences, either spiritual or temporal. The Chapel became a sort of local, better quality, Gretna Green, where runaway couples could be married with the full formalities of the ritual.

Oliver Cromwell may have overlooked this little Chapel, hidden in the hills, but in the Chapter House at Lichfield argument raged. Here was a Chapel within the diocese, but not under its jurisdiction. Every effort was made to rectify this state of affairs but the Vicar at the end of the seventeenth century, the Rev Oldfield, was not easily overcome. He protested that his Chapel was built on Crown land and not subject to the Bishop of Lichfield, moreover his title and rights had been upheld at the time of the Restoration. The Bishop of Lichfield and his henchmen were utterly routed. The marriage fees added some £100 per annum to the Vicar's income, so his privileges were well worth defending.

In 1754, Hardwicke's Marriage Act was passed which was designed to end the scandal of clandestine marriages. It enacted that weddings could only be solemnised after the publication of banns. The Act also laid down that no marriage might be performed except by a clergyman of the Church of England, although Jews and Quakers were exempt. It also provided that minors were to obtain the consent of their parents or guardians. This led to a steady reduction in the number of marriages at Peak Forest. Still later, in 1804, the Vicar's privileges were abolished by a further Act of Parliament. The Chapel was demolished in 1878 and the present Church erected by the Duke of Devonshire.

Early one morning in the mid-seventeenth century, a young couple variously described as coming from the south of England or out of Scotland, travelling on horseback, called at the Royal Oak in Stoney Middleton. The appearance of such a wealthy couple drew the attention of villagers and many gathered to gape at the richly caparisoned horses. The couple called for the ostler but the inn did not live up to its fine name being a mean place at the time, and there was no ostler to be found. A slatternly girl finally opened the door and the young man was surprised to see the state of the inn. The room had not been cleared from the previous night's carousing, and broken furniture lay about the place. Eventually the landlord and his wife were roused and a breakfast prepared for the couple.

While they were eating the wily hostess made it her business to eavesdrop on their conversation and learned that their names were Allan and Clara. (This certainly rings true for there is nothing Peakland folks like better than to know each other's business.) She also overheard Allan asking Clara why she was so downcast. She told him that during the night she had a terrible dream in which she saw her brother who had died twelve years previously, and worse still, that later in the dream the couple were attacked by five men of brutal appearance and cruelly murdered. Allan had done his best to reassure his companion but nothing he could say could raise her spirits.

Having dined, Allan asked the landlord to prepare their horses and for directions as to the best way to the Chapel at Peak Forest. The landlord directed them through Castleton and the Winnats.

"Hold there, a moment", you cry, "If I was going from Stoney Middleton to Peak Forest, I wouldn't dream of going by such a roundabout route. Certainly not, I would go straight up Middleton Dale along the A623." Quite so, but in the mid-eighteenth century the High Peak was far wilder than today, goods traffic being restricted largely to packhorse trains. Burdett's map of 1762-7 shows the Woodhead Turnpike Road to the north, but the earliest coach road developed from the packhorse ways was turnpiked from Manchester to Chapel-en-le-Frith in 1724. In 1749 this was extended through Sparrowpit to Peak Forest, but the linking turnpike through Sparrowpit to Sheffield was not promoted and authorised until 1758. The 1758 turnpike followed the packhorse route up the one in five gradient of the Winnats.

Originally this forbidding ravine was aptly known as Windgates, a name which gradually became corrupted to Winyates and finally contracted to Winnats. Even today, the Winnats Pass can be a wild lonely place with great limestone crags towering on either side and the wind howling through. The very place for cut-throats to lie in wait for the unwary traveller.

On reaching Castleton around ten o'clock the couple ordered a meal at an inn and while eating they were spotted by four uncouth, savage looking lead miners through the open door of another room. This gang were the worse for drink and the landlord ordered them out because of their behaviour and chiefly because they had no money left. The four, whose names have been passed down as James Ashton, Francis Butler, Nicholas Cock and Thomas Hall, called at other taverns along the village street, but were refused admittance. When last seen they were heading towards the Odin Mine where they worked. The lead miners had spotted the loaded saddlebags of the young couple, which had been carried into the inn, and they decided to deprive the owners of the contents.

As they approached the Odin Mine they met John Bradshaw, a blacksmith who also worked there and forced him by threats to accompany them. The five then set out for the Winnats Pass to lie in wait for the travellers.

Around noon, Allan and Clara left Castleton to complete the last few miles to Peak Forest intending to marry at the Chapel. When they entered the narrow defile of the Winnats, the villainous crew rushed out, Hall and Butler seized the horses bridles and threatened to kill the horses with their pickaxes. Hall dragged Allan to the ground where the others grabbed hold of him and dragged him to a nearby barn. Next they dragged Clara after him. Having robbed the pair of some £200 and other valuables it dawned on the drink besotted minds of these scoundrels that the shadow of the gallows was hanging over them and they decided to do away with their victims to dispose of witnesses.

Guessing their murderous intent, Allan rushed desperately at them but was overpowered and struck down with a blow to the head from a miner's pickaxe and next one of the villains slit the girl's throat. After this shocking deed, the murderers divided the booty between them and then hid in the barn until darkness. They returned the following night and putting the bodies into sacks, carried them away and buried them nearby.

The day after the bodies had been thus rudely interred, the horses were discovered, still bridled and saddled in a forest adjoining the Winnats and brought to Castleton. The horses were immediately recognised and the notion that something dreadful had befallen the couple spread around. One suggestion was that they had been thrown into the Eldon Hole but no trace of their bodies was ever found there. It is unlikely that the names of the victims will ever be discovered. Had the crime been committed on the return journey their names would have been recorded in the Register of Foreign Marriages at Peak Forest.

The horses were later removed from Castleton to Chatsworth House as waifs, the Duke of Devonshire being tenant to the Duchy of Lancaster for the manorial rights of Castleton. The trappings were kept at Chatsworth for many years so that they could be claimed by relatives. The parents of Allan and Clara must have had no idea of where or how they had disappeared or there would surely have been a greater search for them and their murderers.

There was no positive evidence at the time of the murders to implicate the culprits but dark hints were whispered around Castleton. James Ashton bought horses with his share of the proceeds of the crime, but the horses died in rapid succession. He is alleged to have said, *"I have always a beautiful lady with me - she rides my horse."*

Nicholas Cock's daughter went to church not long afterwards in a rich silk dress which was the talk of the village. The perpetrators of the crime would never have been known for certain if the last survivor of them, James Ashton, after lying on his death bed for ten weeks, had not confessed that he and four other villagers were responsible. He died the same day, the only one to die a natural death. According to local tradition, the rest of the murderers met terrible ends. William Wood says, *"The hand of God found them out."*

Nicholas Cock fell from a precipice in the Winnats close to the scene of the crime and was killed instantly. A heavy stone fell from the hillside and John Bradshaw was killed on the spot to the amazement of witnesses. Francis Butler went mad and died in a miserable condition after several unsuccessful attempts at suicide. Thomas Hall hanged himself.

There are several conflicting accounts of the bodies being discovered later. In one they were discovered by a party of miners sinking a shaft, and the bodies buried in Castleton churchyard. I can find no record of such a burial in the Parish Records and although such records are often incomplete, one would expect an event of this nature to be entered.

In another account the bodies were flung into the Speedwell Mine. This mine is situated at the lower entrance to the Winnats, and according to Bulmer's Derbyshire was not opened until 1770 which should safely rule out this explanation. The Reporter for September 3rd 1921, stated that the previous weekend's discovery of human remains at Castleton had aroused "widespread interest as to the story the remains may hide." The entry was:

A Peak mystery; human skeletons found in Winnats Pass: Are they murder victims?" The story continued:

"The skeletons were found on Tray (Treak) Cliff by men working for West and Company of Liverpool, who are getting fluorspar. They are those of a man and woman, and they are remarkably preserved. Mr Taylor, the High Peak Coroner, was informed of the discovery. He did not hold an inquest, and ordered that the remains be buried. In Castleton the bones are believed to be those of the victims of the Winnats murder of 1758."

"Thus the untimely end of innocence was avenged by the never failing hand of retributive justice; and the punishment of human laws, though seldom ever evaded, was supplied by that watchful eye which can never be deceived."

S. Evans J.P.

When William Wood wrote his first account of the murders it was not well received in Castleton by the descendants of those accused. Indeed when Wood later visited that village he had to be taken into the Nag's Head to be safe from the mob who were adopting an ugly and menacing attitude. He had to make a safe exit by a rear window.

I worked at one time with a skilled stonemason who came from Castleton and he said that seventy years ago the crimes were still talked of in hushed whispers. Should you attempt to make enquiries about the murders in Castleton, do not be surprised if you

The Royal Oak at Stoney Middleton, as it appears today.

Winnats Pass.

receive evasive or even surly answers, after all, you could easily be talking to descendants of the killers.

Among the burials in the Parish Register at Castleton are the following entries

James Ashton, October 18th 1778 (the man who confessed).

Thomas Hall, June 9th 1751.

Thomas Hall, May 28th 1753.

Nicholas Cock, buryd 29th December 1766.

John Bradshaw, August 30th 1774.

The surname of Francis Butler does not appear, but as he went mad he might be buried elsewhere. Hall is a common name in the district and the two listed might not have been involved. The murderer Thomas Hall, committed suicide and could have been buried at some crossroads.

An interesting postcript to this sombre tale is that during World War Two, the Rev Williams-Morrison, Vicar at Peak Forest and formerly curate at Saint Lukes', Glossop, reintroduced a modified form of the Gretna Green marriage at his church for young people in the services who could not meet the residency requirements.

Disgraceful Affair - Female Pugilists: 10.10.1874

Martha Mullings, of Higher Bibbington, was charged with assaulting Alice Higginbotham, who appeared in court with both her eyes blacked. Mrs Higginbotham said on the 26th ult. between nine and ten in the morning, the defendant challenged to fight all the women in the row two at a time. A witness saw them fighting one round, when she got to them Mrs Mullings was standing over the other and saying, "Get up if you want any more."

The Chairman said it was one of the worst cases that ever he heard. Dismissed, each to pay costs.

1874: Fire at Litton Mill

Derbyshire was involved in the Industrial Revolution from its earliest years. Thomas Catchett was silk throwing in a water driven mill by the Derwent at Derby in 1702. Richard Arkwright's first mill was built at Cromford in 1771 and he built others soon afterwards. Arkwright's mill has become a popular tourist attraction, but what is less well known is that there were many smaller mills situated in remote valleys where there was a copious flow of water to supply the motive power to drive the machinery. Many of these early mills were little bigger than a cottage and some of them were converted into short rows of cottages when they became no longer financially viable.

The fast running Pennine streams held the advantage of cheap power until the development of the steam engine caused production to move closer to the coal fields of Lancashire and Yorkshire and the old mills fell into decay.

Keep your eyes open for tell-tale signs of these lost mills as you travel through quiet corners of the region. It may just be a weir across a stream which appears to have no reason for existence until you discover a goyt (or leat), leading to a lodge which once stored the water to drive the waterwheel. The dam may well be broken and the stones of the mill carted away to be used elsewhere, but it is often possible to make out where it once stood by the rectangular mound that remains. Other indications are the traces of wheel pits, boiler and engine mountings, and roads having no obvious reason for existence. A village as small as Rowarth could once claim six mills and a walk along Rowarth Dell will soon make clear how small a stream was necessary to power these early factories.

In these ecologically aware times, water might seem an ideal source of power, but it created its share of problems. To ensure sufficient water to drive the water wheel during the day, the sluices would be closed at night and the mill lodges filled to their maximum capacity. In steep sided valleys with fast flowing streams this was not usually necessary, but in flatter country farmers were far from pleased to have their pastures turned into marshes by this nightly flooding. Then there was the ever present danger of poorly constructed dams bursting.

Litton Mill, by the River Wye, was a larger establishment whose main claim to fame, prior to the fire, was the shocking treatment of pauper apprentices sent there by the Churchwardens and Overseers of the Poor of London parishes at the end of the eighteenth and beginning of the nineteenth centuries. (If you have not already read *'A Memoir of Robert Blincoe'*, make it your business to do so. Some academics have tried to write off Blincoe's tale as mere propaganda, but academics as a group are not noted for their experience of industry.)

Some indication of the size of Litton Mill in 1874, can be deduced from the information that it was four stories high, twenty windows long and four windows wide. This suggests that it was 200 feet long by 40 feet wide since mills were built to a fairly regular pattern.

This account of a serious mill fire gives considerable insight into working conditions one hundred and twenty years ago. By 1874, the situation had certainly improved but the working day still commenced at six in the morning. At 7.00 am on Friday 4th September, a fire started on the top floor of the mill caused by the overheating of a headstock on a pair of mules. There were no ball races used on these machines and the shafts would rotate in brass, bronze, or even cast iron bearings which were lubricated by the intermittent drip from inverted oil bottles or wick feeds. In the event of the failure of these crude lubrication methods, the bearing would overheat rapidly and seize up or throw out a shower of sparks. It was vital that the oiler and greaser kept the bearings under constant watch. The need for constant oiling resulted in the machines being covered in oil which eventually found its way to the floor where it soaked right into the floorboards. The air was full of cotton fluff and dust which adhered

Litton Mill.

Litton Mill with examples of old gearing.

to the oily machinery and collected on top of beams and in crevices in the walls. After a few years the place would be like a tinder box. It needed only a spark for fire to spread through the building at tremendous speed.

Sparks from the overheated bearing fell onto the oily wooden floor which was quickly alight. At the outset a bucket of water dashed on the flames might have quenched the fire, but there was no proper provision for tackling a blaze, certainly nothing as sophisticated as a sprinkler system to keep a fire under control. There was a manual fire engine on the premises but it was out of repair and unfit to do anything.

The hands did what they could to fight the blaze, carrying buckets of water from the river, many throwing them vainly at the growing inferno, but the flames raced across the oil impregnated floors as if they were covered in paraffin. The building was old and oil had been soaking into the boards for years until it was dripping through to the floors beneath in places. The valiant efforts of the hands were useless and soon the flames took hold of the roof which fell in with a tremendous crash. Workmen from all around the area rushed to the scene but they were powerless to stay the conflagration. A newspaper account of the disaster stated that six fire engines could not have saved the building even if they had arrived within minutes of its commencement.

A railway line through the Wye Valley was opened in 1863, and it is about six miles by rail from Litton Mill to Buxton and rather more by road. The Buxton Fire Brigade came galloping onto the scene at half past eight, which was a creditable performance in an age before the invention of the telephone. Even if a train had been passing as the fire broke out and been able to convey the dire news to Buxton it can have been no easy task to turn out the Brigade and haul a horse-drawn fire engine up hill and down dale on the roads of the time. Some stretches are still narrow and dangerous today. The method of braking horse drawn vehicles was by forcing a wooden block or scotch against the iron rim of the wheel so the risks involved in travelling rapidly downhill are not hard to imagine.

The Buxton Fire Brigade was established in 1863 with twelve members, and by the time of the Litton Mill fire these had grown to twenty five. They were all volunteers and were called out by the ringing of a bell. In addition to assembling the firemen, horses would have to be obtained from local carriers to pull the appliance as the Brigade could not afford the luxury of having its own team standing by in case of a fire. This may seem an haphazard way to run a fire brigade, but Buxton was well ahead of many towns of a similar size who relied on the fire engines of local mill owners.

There was little the Fire Brigade could do with their manually operated pump when they arrived on the scene, but the office and store room, which still contained some stock, was saved by playing the hoses on them. The mill proper was completely gutted. No lives were lost in the disaster, but lads lost their boots because they worked barefoot. The men lost their jackets and the women their bonnets and cloaks. Cotton mills were so hot and humid that many worked in little more than their underwear. No cloakrooms or drying facilities in those days, you just hung your jacket on a nail in the wall or on the end of a machine. The most prized possession of many a workman was his watch and there were several who lost their lives in similar fires because they went back into the building in an attempt to save them.

There were some three hundred hands employed in the mill who we are told had become very attached to their masters as the result of kind treatment. Let us hope that this was true after the brutish regime of Ellice Needham in earlier years. The loss of three hundred jobs would severely affect the locality until the mill was rebuilt. Some of the workers found employment at Cressbrook Mill, a little further down the Wye Valley, but others had to move as far as Stockport. The Litton Mill was owned by W.C. Moore who also owned Bamford Mill. Mr Moore was also a Justice of the Peace who used to sit at the Petty Sessions at Chapel-en-le-Frith. At that time Justices of the Peace were recruited exclusively from the old landed gentry and from the newly enriched leaders of industry, hardly an ideal group to facilitate the work of the totally inadequate number of Factory Inspectors.

Fortunately the mill was insured with the Phoenix, Globe and Lancashire Insurance Company and the damage was estimated at £20,000. The insurance companies of the day did more to improve safety with regard to fires, boiler explosions and accidents than the pitifully few Factory Inspectors.

The first mill was built on the site in 1782. After the fire the mill was rebuilt and in 1895 was used for cotton doubling. There are several mill buildings still standing on the site, which is worth a visit to inspect the methods of construction used and the samples of old machinery on display outside.

Train theft 16.5.1874

On Thursday evening, the engine driver, stoker and guard of a goods train were found to be drunk on passing Bakewell Station on the Midland Railway. They were at once removed from the train and fresh staff sent for. The result of their disgraceful conduct was that they became occupants of the Bakewell Police Cell in short order. It transpired later that a quarter cask of sherry had been sent from Manchester to Bakewell and the accused had sampled its contents; some four and a quarter gallons having gone astray. The train had to be shunted onto a siding so as to allow the London express to pass through Bakewell. It appears that the method employed by the culprits was to bore a hole in the cask and then run off a quantity of the liquor into bottles with the intention of plugging the hole afterwards to conceal the theft.

At the Bakewell Petty Sessions: John White, engine driver, of Derby; Charles Elson, fireman, also of Derby, and William Heels, guard, of Rowsley were charged with the theft of property of the Midland Railway company while in transit by train. John White was discharged as, although he had been the worse for drink, it had not been proved that he had been near the truck containing the cask. The other two were sentenced to appear at the next Derby Assizes where Elson received 2 months, and Heels 6 months imprisonment, both with hard labour.

James Brindley

James Brindley was born in 1716 in the hamlet of Tunstead near Buxton. His father, a husbandman, was more interested in sport than work and as a result the family were too poor for James to receive anything more than the most rudimentary schooling. Considerable emphasis has been laid on the fact that he was semi-literate and spoke with a rough Derbyshire accent. Doubtless he was the eighteenth century equivalent of the boy who shows little aptitude for schoolwork but teachers confidently predict will 'Probably be good with his hands.' It is quite incredible that such nonsense is still mouthed.

By the age of seventeen his family had moved to Leek and he was apprenticed for seven years to Abraham Bennet, a wheelwright and millwright in the village of Sutton near Macclesfield. Young James tended to be the butt for his workmates jokes because of his persistence in working out his own solutions to problems regardless of their traditional methods. With his perseverance, he gradually began to leave the other workmen behind, which did nothing to add to his popularity. He was very conscientious seeking perfection in everything he made. This did not always meet with the approval of his master who was known to complain that his work might last too long and never need repair which was not in the best interests of the business.

The trade of millwright had grown from the need for men to build and maintain windmills, waterwheels, and similar devices. These men had to be skilled in the working of wood and metals, have an understanding of the trades of masons and bricklayers, and be capable of working on their own initiative. One skill in particular they had to master and that was the job of moving heavy items without the assistance of power cranes, stacker trucks, or the like. With the Industrial Revolution leading to new machines and engines, men with Brindley's ability to tackle problems which had never been met before were at a premium.

Abraham Bennet obtained the contract to install an engine in a paper mill and was having great difficulty in completing the job. One Monday morning, Brindley failed to turn up for work on time and Bennet was beginning to despair of being able to complete the job. But Brindley was not the man to be beaten with such a problem. During the weekend, he had walked to the site of the mill engine which was being copied, studied it carefully and then walked back, and on arriving late at work, showed Bennet where he was going wrong. He must have had a remarkably retentive memory to study a mechanism and then reproduce it correctly without the aid of a drawing or any written instructions. Not a bad showing for an illiterate rustic. It was said that when faced with a difficult problem, he would take to his bed and lie there until he had thought it through to a satisfactory solution.

In 1742 Brindley started his own business in Leek where among other work he was employed in building flint mills for the pottery trade. The flint was required to make new qualities of white glazed ware which were known as stoneware. This work for the pottery trade led Brindley to meet the famous potter Josiah Wedgwood.

Brindley was a millwright who was prepared to tackle a wide variety of work. The coal pits at Clifton in Lancashire were troubled with drainage difficulties. In 1752, Brindley solved the problem by excavating a 600 yard underground channel and moving the water with a waterwheel powered by the River Irwell. Each of these successful ventures added to his stature as an engineer and inventor. In addition to this work he built models of atmospheric engines. Some of the early ones were constructed partly of wood, but with perseverance he eventually built an engine which performed to his satisfaction.

Francis Egerton, the third Duke of Bridgewater wanted to transport, economically, the coal from his mines at Worsley to supply the growing number of cotton mills in Manchester. As a young man, the Duke had been on a grand tour of Europe where he had been impressed by the 150 mile long Grand Canal of Languedoc which had been completed in 1681. It may have been this experience which led to him financing the construction of the first English canal of economic importance. The Mersey and Irwell Navigation Company refused to let him have access to the River Irwell so he determined to build his own canal for which he obtained an Act of Parliament in 1759.

In 1759, Brindley was introduced to the Duke of Bridgewater by the Duke's Agent, John Gilbert. The Duke hired him to build a 10 mile canal to transport coal from the mines at Worsley to the centre of Manchester. Although the Duke was a wealthy man, he many times ran into financial difficulties before the project was completed.

Brindley's solution to the problem included a subterranean channel, extending from the barge basin at the head of the canal into the mines, and the Barton Aqueduct, which carried the canal over the River Irwell. The idea of carrying a canal over a river was greeted with amazement and even derision, but on completion it worked without a hitch and people came from miles around to see barges sailing above the river. There were no locks on the Bridgewater Canal; Brindley following the contour line. It would have been possible to follow a shorter route by using locks but Brindley at this stage in his career preferred to stick to methods he knew would work. Lock construction required the skills of masons, carpenters, blacksmiths and foremen, and the knowledge to supervise their work. Since this was the first scheme of its kind in England, such skilled men were not easily found.

Brindley Mill, Leek.

Brindley's stone-built Barton Aqueduct 1761.

In his later canals, Brindley would use locks and drive tunnels. Brindley's Harecastle Tunnel on the Grand Trunk Canal was the first canal tunnel in England. It was a crude affair when compared with what was to follow, but it is much easier to improve on the work of others than to be first in the field. Nevertheless considerable ingenuity was shown, and when coal seams were struck during the boring of the Harecastle Tunnel, miners excavated the coal which was carried away by barge.

Where suitable clay was found it was used for lining the canal with clay puddle, or turned into bricks. If clay is mixed thoroughly with water by tramping underfoot to the right consistency it becomes impervious to water. This 'puddled' clay was used to line canals and mill ponds and the workman in charge of the process was known as the puddle-tinter. It could well be that the word puddled, meaning stupid could be derived from this occupation, the argument being that you had to be puddled to do it.

The canal running from the mines at Worsley straight into the centre of Manchester meant that coal could be delivered to the fast growing cotton mills at a competitive price. The price fell from seven pence to three pence per hundredweight, helping Manchester to expand at an even faster rate and the Duke to profit handsomely from his venture.

Canals need a water supply even when they have no locks as there will be losses through evaporation and seepage. Brindley used the water which was constantly being drained from the Duke's mines. The coal was run out of the mines in trucks which were loaded directly into the barges. At the Manchester terminus at the foot of Castle Hill purchasers were faced with the daunting prospect of a weary tramp to the top with their loads, so Brindley solved this problem by extending the canal into the hill and sinking a vertical shaft down to meet it. A water wheel was employed to power a hoist at the top which raised the trucks straight from the barges to the top of the hill. He thus saved unnecessary handling at each end of the route.

The success of the Bridgewater Canal encouraged similar projects. The Grand Trunk Canal, penetrating the central ridge of England by the Harecastle Tunnel; the Staffordshire and Worcestershire; the Coventry; the Oxford; the old Birmingham and the Chesterfield canals, were all designed and, with one exception, executed by Brindley. In all, he was responsible for a network of canals totalling about 360 miles. In addition to supervising all these undertakings, James Brindley appeared before parliamentary committees to help get the necessary Acts for canal construction passed. He may not have had a great command of English but when stuck for words he would produce a piece of chalk and make a diagram on the floor for the benefit of the Members of Parliament or even give a demonstration of how to puddle clay.

These improvements in communications helped to foster the Industrial Revolution since it was now possible to move steam engines and boilers as well as coal and building materials. It is incredible that Brindley, a self made engineer, undertook all his works without written calculations or drawings, leaving no records for posterity, except the works themselves.

James Brindley died on 30th August, 1772 at his home in Turnhurst Staffordshire. A memorial to Brindley was erected in Wormhill. Bulmer's Derbyshire describes it as follows: *Embowered in a grove of holly and yew trees is a well, surmounted by a monument, triangular in shape, and about 12 feet high on which is inscribed: 1875. In memory of James Brindley, civil engineer, born in this parish, A.D. 1716.'*

The memorial and well are still there. The yews and hollies have since been augmented by varieties of cupressus.

Brindley Memorial, Wormhill.

Gentlemen of the Road

Highwaymen and footpads must have existed as long as there were roads and people travelling along them with goods of value. The highwayman, as popularly portrayed with his cocked hat, high boots, black mask and armoury of pistols, only made his appearance after the English Civil Wars during the second half of the 17th century, and his reign lasted until the end of the 18th century. Many who had lost their property during the wars tried to recover their losses by theft, and of course there were many unhappy with the outcomes of the war who were now well armed as a result. The flintlock pistol which was more reliable then the wheel-lock and matchlock pistols which it superseded, made the highwayman a dangerous robber for the average traveller to tackle. A further encouragement, at a time when the attainment of high office was seen as an opportunity for personal enrichment, was that these rogues could argue that they were only trying to emulate their betters. The one thing they all shared in common was a wish to live the life of a gentleman without the discomfort of doing an honest day's work. They much preferred to stop a coach of lonely travellers on the highway and force them to hand over their money and valuables at the point of a brace of pistols.

Before banking services were properly established, wealthy folks were forced to carry their valuables with them. The really wealthy travelled under the guard of a band of tough servants, armed, and ready to shoot on sight, or to capture highwaymen or footpads. The firearms of the day were unreliable and inaccurate and highwaymen made it their business to have several loaded pistols at the ready in case of a 'flash in the pan'. Many travellers hesitated to use firearms in their own defence because they thought, not without good reason, that the highwaymen were more expert in their use. These scoundrels were not in the habit of advertising their activities or whereabouts for obvious reasons, and further, their exploits have been embroidered by writers so that the true extent of their handiwork is hard to unravel.

In his History of England, Macaulay tells us; '*It was necessary to the success and even the safety of the highwayman that he should be a bold and skilful rider and that his manners and appearance should be such as suited the master of a fine horse. He therefore held an aristocratic position in the community of thieves, appeared at fashionable coffee houses and gaming houses, and betted with men of quality on the race-ground. Sometimes, indeed, he was a man of good family and education. A romantic interest therefore attached, and perhaps still attaches, to the names of freebooters of this class. The vulgar eagerly drank in tales of their ferocity and audacity, of their occasional acts of generosity and good nature, of their amours, of their miraculous escapes, of their desperate struggles, and of their manly bearing at the bar and in the cart.*'

One problem in discovering the true details of the activities of local highwaymen is that the records of the Quarter Sessions become more difficult to decipher the further back you go. Yet another difficulty is that these were hardly the fellows to fill in their tax returns accurately. Hence it is not surprising that I have failed to find written evidence for the existence of Black Harry who seemingly ended his days on the gibbet at Wardlow Mires. He is reputed to have preyed on packhorse trains and lonely travellers as they wended their way across the moors in the Wardlow and Longstone area. However, there still exists a Black Harry Lane, Black Harry Gate, and a Black Harry House once stood nearby (SK 203745), so he must have been real enough to have been commemorated in this fashion.

With William, or John, Nevison, perhaps better known as 'Swift Nick Nevison' or the 'Derbyshire Dick Turpin' we are on much firmer ground. A scourge of the district years before Turpin started on his infamous career, many of his exploits were later attributed to Turpin. The celebrated ride to York in 1665, being the best known. Nevison was a man who would cheerfully ride across the Derwent in mid-winter when the waters were in spate or plunge down some steep craggy hillside to elude pursuit. Like Turpin on Black Bess he would clear any turnpike gate that blocked his way.

John Nevison is reputed to have been born at Pontefract in 1639 to a respectable family. An inspection of the International Genealogical Index of The Mormon Church Saints reveals that the surname Nevison is rare in Derbyshire but comparatively common in Yorkshire. The only birth I have discovered which meets the requirements of our highwayman is that of John Nevison, son of Thomas Nevison born in the parish of Harewood on 25th March 1633. If this is correct then he had a twin, Thomas, christened on the same day and two younger brothers Richard and Robert. An examination of the parish registers for Pontefract might clear up the matter. Wherever he was born, he is alleged to have begun his career of crime by stealing his father's money and his schoolmaster's horse. To leave no trace, he killed the horse before entering London.

Shortly afterwards Nevison moved to Holland where he continued the same way of life until he was arrested for thieving and imprisoned. He later escaped and served for a time with English regiments serving in Flanders before deserting and returning to England. With Yorkshire as a base he set himself up as an extortioner in company with two liked minded men, Thomas Tankard and Edward Bracy.

Turning to Macaulay's account once more we learn that it was related of Nevison, *'that he levied a quarterly tribute on all the northern drovers, and in return, not only spared them himself, but protected them against all other thieves; that he demanded purses in the most courteous manner; that he gave largely to the poor what he had taken from the rich.'*

If a highwayman was to keep up his nefarious ways for any length of time he had to be able to count on the local people keeping quiet. This object was achieved partly through the threat of dire consequences for anyone foolish enough to inform on his hiding places and partly through acquiring a Robin Hood reputation by passing on some of his booty to the more needy. By such means were Nevison and the like able to operate undetected by the law for lengthy periods.

To return to the 'Ride to York'; John Nevison stopped and robbed a gentleman near Gadshill early one morning in 1665. Realising that he had been recognised by his victim, Nevison crossed the Thames at Gravesend and galloped across the country all day arriving in York just before sundown. Quickly changing out of his travel stained clothing he hurried to the public bowling green where he made it his business to be noticed by as many prominent citizens as possible. Fortunately for Nevison, the Lord Mayor of the City was present that evening. When charged with the Gadshill robbery he was able to call on the Lord Mayor to testify as to the day and time when he was in York and was duly acquitted on the grounds that he could not possibly have been in two such distant places on the same day. There seems to be an element of truth in this story, although no doubt it has been improved in the telling. King Charles II, on hearing of the exploit, asked to meet Nevison and after christening him 'Swift Nick' bestowed a royal pardon on him.

Arrested more than once, he managed reprieves and escapes, but finally, after shooting a butcher named Fletcher who tried to arrest him near Leeds, a generous reward was offered by the government for his capture. This led to his apprehension shortly afterwards when he was betrayed by the mistress of the Three Houses Inn at Sandal near Wakefield. He was tried and hanged at York on 15th March 1685. If his birth date is correct, then he lived to the grand old age of 45, an achievement not matched by many engaged in his profession. The most often related story of his exploits is as follows:

One market day Nevison mixed with the crowds at Bakewell making a careful note of any who appeared to have done well in disposing of their beasts or other wares. Among those who had taken cattle to market was a farmer from Padley who needed the cash because rent-day was approaching and when he had sold all his animals for a fair price, he retired to a tavern for a celebratory drink before setting out for home. Nevison made it his business to join him and after befriending him and sharing drinks together the pair set off to travel together. The cunning Nevison had found that the farmer was headed for Padley some six and a half miles distant, and announced that his journey lay in the same direction as he was heading for Sheffield.

The farmer noted that Nevison was riding a fine horse, an essential possession for the successful highwayman, and commented on it. Nevison replied to the effect that they were travelling in dangerous times and that a good steed was needed if one's possessions were to be safe from footpads and others of the same ilk along the road.

The pair travelled up hill and down dale, through Hassop and on through Calver Sough, until they reached to the top of the long rise beyond and stopped to rest their horses. Suddenly Nevison's friendly attitude changed and he pointed his loaded pistol straight at the farmer's breast.

The farmer pleaded with Nevison explaining that the cattle had only been sold to meet his rent which was due in ten days time, otherwise he would have kept them. Without the money to meet the rent and with a large family to keep he would be utterly ruined. The highwayman would have none of it and the farmer was forced to hand over his bag of gold or forfeit his life.

As Nevison placed the stolen money inside his coat he said, *"As it is rent money, it shall be repaid. But present cash is lasting aid, and needs must when the devil drives. Hark ye farmer, it is yet ten days to Michaelmas, and on the eve of the saint, holy water and blessings on his memory, I'll be with you."* and with these parting words he spurred his horse away in the direction of Eyam and was gone from the poor farmer's sight in a matter of seconds.

It so happened that at this time a sentry box had been erected on the narrow Grindleford Bridge as a protection for the area and so that a quarantine could be imposed on the movement of cattle on account of the murrain which was afflicting the Derbyshire flocks and herds. As the days passed and Michaelmas drew nearer, the farmer became ever more despondent as he wondered if the highwayman would keep his word and the money be repaid. On Michaelmas Eve at the stroke of midnight the farmer was aroused by the sound of firearms and presently a horse came galloping up

Black Harry Lane.

Dick Turpin eluding his pursuers by clearing the turnpike gate on Black Bess.

the road which led to the bridge at Grindleford and as it passed the farmer's humble
dwelling he heard the crash of the window panes and frame as something was flung
violently against them before the sounds and sight of the horse and rider were lost in
Padley woods.

It appears that bold Nevison had again visited Bakewell Market and lightened the
pockets of several successful traders. In his flight he had been hotly pursued as far as
Grindleford Bridge. Nevison avoided the sentry box by fording the stream and the
sentinel, roused by the sounds of pursuit, fired at the dim figure, but his aim was not
sure, perhaps because he recognised the highwayman. Nevison fired his pistol in return,
with as little effect, made the opposite bank and escaped.

The farmer thought it poor payment to have his windows and casement smashed;
surely this was not the promised gold to pay the rent? But to his surprise there lying on
the floor was his old canvas money bag which when opened was found to contain, not
only the sum of which he had been robbed, but an extra guinea wrapped in a slip of
paper, on which was written, "Interest for the loan of rent money."

Let us turn now to the notorious Dick Turpin. In June 1737, a proclamation
appeared in the London Gazette offering a reward of £200 to any person or persons who
shall discover the whereabouts of Dick Turpin so that he may be apprehended and
convicted. With such a large reward on his head Turpin could trust no-one and was
forced to flee from the London area and later turned up in Welton to the west of Hull in
the East Riding. He set himself up as a gentleman horse dealer in October 1737 under
the name of John Palmer, and from his base in Welton he would range far afield, stealing
horses, later selling them at very reasonable prices.

There are good reasons for thinking that on at least one of these thieving
excursions he may have travelled down the Longdendale valley. A Tintwistle gentleman
is the proud possessor an old anvil which he claims was used by one of his ancestors, a
local blacksmith, to shoe Turpin's horse. The work was carried out at pistol point and
the shoes were put on backwards to deceive any pursuer! Yet another Tintwistle resident
claims to have the hammer used to knock the nails in. Perhaps the best evidence of all
comes from the collective memories of children who pass on stories from one to the
other. Before it was demolished some years ago, small boys in Tintwistle could show
you the small stone building where Turpin stabled his horse. It had a door which opened
in two halves and stood by the main road on the cobbled way up to the stocks, opposite
the lane which winds up round the back of the Church. Reversing the horses shoes, or
replacing them with circular ones were certainly tricks used by highwaymen. Although
there is no record of Turpin operating as a highwayman in the district, he could have
been pursued here if suspected of horse theft.

Whatever the truth behind these stories, Turpin was eventually caught after an
incident in which he shot a cockerel which belonged to his landlord. As a result 'John
Palmer' was arrested and eventually Turpin's true identity revealed, and in due course

he was sentenced to death. On the morning of 7th April 1739, Turpin stepped into the cart which was to convey him to the Knavesmire outside York where the gallows awaited. Attired in a fine new coat and attended by poor men he had hired as mourners, Turpin was watched by a huge crowd as the cart slowly passed to its destination. Turpin stood in the cart, bowing and doffing his cap to ladies of quality. He stood on the platform joking with the hangman for some minutes then the rope was tightened round his neck. Turpin motioned the hangman away before throwing himself off.

His body was buried in the graveyard of St George's Church, York, but in the early hours of the next morning bodysnatchers were discovered in the churchyard preparing to carry the body away to the surgeons. The news spread like wildfire and the mob, determined to prevent the body falling into the hands of the dissectors, were soon on the scene in strength. Finally it was reburied in the same grave, but this time the coffin was partly filled with lime. The inscription on his gravestone reads "I.R. 1739. R.T. aged 28." (He was actually 33). Don't fail to visit it next time you go to York.

Highwaymen thought nothing of holding up a coach under the very gibbet on which swung one of their own kind with the tattered rags of his clothes still clinging to his bones as they rattled in the wind. The successful ones showed great courage and cunning in carrying out their nefarious exploits, but almost inevitably gave themselves away, drawing attention to themselves by failing to pay debts to businessmen or by boasting of their wealth and activities. Many of them stole vast sums over a short period of time, but spent it almost as quickly on mistresses and gambling as they tried to live the life of a moneyed young blood. Although they knew that they were almost certainly headed for the gallows, almost all of them persisted until they were taken, but some few did disappear after a life on the road presumably to some mundane occupation in an out of the way spot. Few escaped for long, and many highwaymen were "turned off" the gallows in their twenties.

In addition to these well known villains there were plenty of lesser rogues who ended their lives on the gallows at Derby for highway robbery: On 2nd March 1738, Richard Woodward (he dressed himself in his shroud and walked to the place of execution which is reported as being both in Derby and Bakewell); on 9th April 1740 William Dolphin; 1763, J.Perry and Amos Mason; on 14th August 1801, Powell and Drummond, and perhaps the last, on April 2nd 1819, Thomas Hopkinson after cheating the gallows on a previous occasion by turning King's Evidence, was hanged for stealing a whip from a coach.

The heyday of the highwayman was over by the end of the 18th century, due in part to improvement in banking services so that travellers no longer needed to carry large amounts of cash, and the relentless efforts of honest magistrates and the Bow Street Runners. The enclosure of land also deprived the highwaymen of hideaways and now the only reminder we have is the highwayman's knot, which enabled him to release his tethered horse in an instant.

Resurrectionists at Large

Thomas Statham, who died at Tideswell in 1702, might well have been afraid that his body would end up in the hands of the surgeons. He was buried in a vault at Tideswell Church in a 'tinned coffin which he had by him for many years. It had twenty six locks upon it, all locked with one key, which according to his request was cast away after his interment.' He may well have had cause to fear this fate because the stealing of fresh bodies for the use of surgeons was not unknown at this early date. In 1740 George Ashmore was executed for coining and the following day his body was buried at Sutton-on-the-Hill, only to be stolen by the resurrection men.

The precaution taken by Thomas Statham in keeping a coffin ready in ample time reminds me of another gentleman in the Penistone district, who is still very much alive, who took advantage of the outbreak of Dutch Elm disease some years ago to have his coffin made while plenty of cheap timber was available.

It was the Napoleonic Wars that gave the ghastly trade of the bodysnatchers, resurrectionists, or 'sack 'em up men', as they were variously called, its principal boost. Large numbers of surgeons were required for service with the greatly expanded Army and Navy. From the time of Henry VIII the only human bodies available for examination were those of executed criminals, and although there was an unholy crop of these, the supply was never equal to the demand. The only source of bodies for the surgeons to practice their profession on was that of criminals hanged within the confines of the county. Even in an age when the death penalty was applicable for a wide range of crimes, the supply from this source was totally inadequate and the skills of British surgeons lagged behind those in France and Germany. In the late 18th Century only about 20 people were being hanged a year in London and Middlesex, compared with about 140 early in the 17th century. Only about 200 were hanged each year in the whole of England and Wales.

Most Members of Parliament were reluctant to pass legislation to make more bodies available for the training of surgeons because that would almost certainly lead to public rioting. Instead they preferred to turn a blind eye to the manner in which the schools of surgery obtained their supply of bodies. When the surgeons had finished their grim work, the remnants had to be disposed of and on occasion this led to parts of bodies being dug up by dogs on land nearby. This invariably led to violent riots which more than once ended with the surgeon's premises being burned to the ground.

Initially, medical students and lecturers were quite capable of clambering over churchyard walls to obtain corpses but this became a hazardous business when relatives of the deceased started to mount guard and set broken glass in the top of graveyard walls. It was easier and safer to employ desperate ruffians to carry out this grisly work and a thriving trade grew up which naturally was in the hands of the lowest and most depraved. In 1823 about 800 bodies were supplied to the London students alone. At first a body could be had for about £2, but the price rose eventually as high as £20. The result was that in time men resorted to murder in order to supply fresh corpses and this culminated in the infamous Burke and Hare murders where seventeen victims were smothered and their bodies sold at prices from £10 to £17. For many years there was a widespread belief that men went about remote country lanes in carts with muffled wheels, drawn by horses with muffled shoes, and provided with extra strong sticking plasters which were clapped over the mouths of solitary wayfarers who were never heard of again.

It is easy to imagine the feelings of relatives who were already distressed at losing their loved ones only to find that their bodies had been carried away for the benefit of the surgeons. In some city graveyards close to schools of surgery it was discovered that all the recently buried corpses had been spirited away for the use of the surgeons, often because the sextons were also in their pay. As the extent of the trade grew, fierce battles took place between bodysnatchers and relatives armed with blunderbusses and cutlasses. In churchyards in towns near teaching hospitals, guns operated by tripwire were mounted over bodies and some went so far as to plant explosives in the grave. Another method of thwarting the resurrectionists was to drive stakes crosswise into the sides of the grave so that the lid could not be raised. One subterfuge employed by the sextons was to keep raising the coffin a few inches at a time as they filled the grave so that when they had finished there were only a thin covering of soil and the bodysnatchers could carry out their work in a matter of moments.

The public outrage caused the body snatchers to look further afield in search of easier pickings and many a country churchyard became the object of their attention. Some might say that it is unlikely that the bodysnatchers operated in a country district like the Peak, but before being too certain of this, it is as well to bear in mind that in a spot as remote as Pannal in North Yorkshire it was thought necessary to have a stone weighing over a ton, known as the 'resurrection stone' to lower over the coffin. It was far too heavy to be lifted by two or three men and was hired out at a guinea a fortnight. Rather closer to home, at Bradfield in South Yorkshire there is a Watch House sited near to the graveyard so that a guard could be mounted to deter bodysnatchers. At one time there was thriving trade in importing bodies by boat from Ireland so the High Peak would be in easy reach of determined men who could make far more money by stealing a body by night than by weeks of honest toil.

Just because there is no record of a body being stolen in a particular graveyard is no guarantee that it did not happen. The whole object of the practitioners of this gruesome business was to carry out their work without being caught and with the sexton in league with them it would not be difficult. The true extent of this foul trade can never be accurately assessed because in many cases it was never detected or even suspected. The resurrectionists went to considerable lengths to conceal their clandestine activities. It was generally safer to move a body in daylight since there was less chance of running into the Watch. The resurrectionists would dig out just sufficient earth to get a rope round the body and then drag it from the grave before placing it in a sack and moving it to a place of hiding. The shroud would be stripped from the body and stuffed back into the coffin. The resurrectionists would then return in the cold light of day and calmly trundle the body away in a cart so that it could be delivered to the dissectionists. If the body was moved by night then cart wheels were muffled with sacks to deaden sounds as they trundled through dark city streets.

Magistrates had difficulty in convicting a man for stealing a corpse because there was no property in a dead body so it could not be stolen. On the other hand if a ring or the shroud was taken with the body then the thieves could be severely punished.

One place where these nefarious deeds were discovered was at Hope as the following extracts from the Parish Registers show:-
October 26th 1831, Aged 28, William Radwell, Smalldale. The body stolen same night.
October 2nd 1834, Aged 21, Benjamin Wragg, Bradwell. This body stolen.

These crimes, especially the last, occurred very late when the trade of the resurrectionists had virtually ceased.

One well known example locally is the bodysnatchers grave at Mottram. The father of the dead boy exhibited the empty coffin on the Crown Pole Steps despite the Vicar's objections and had a stone with the following inscription placed over the empty grave:-
In memory of James, son of James and Mary Brierley, of Valley Mill, who died
October 3rd, 1827, in the 15th year of his age.
Though once beneath the ground his corpse was laid,
For use of surgeons it was thence conveyed;
Vain was the scheme to hide the impious theft,
The body taken; shroud and coffin left.
Ye wretches, who pursue this barbarous trade,
Your carcasses in turn may be conveyed,
Like his, to some unfeeling surgeon's room.
Nor can they justly meet a better doom.

In Tideswell there once dwelt a doctor who wished to keep his surgical skills up to the mark, so he employed a gang of local rascals whom he thought he could trust to obtain a body for a spot of practice. Just after midnight, a couple of nights later, these fellows arrived on his doorstep with a body trussed up in a sack.

"Where shall we put the goods?" enquired the suppliers.

"Carry it down into the cellar", ordered the Doctor; so the men dragged the body down into the cellar and dumped it in a corner.

As the bodysnatchers set off back to a local tavern, the richer by the princely sum of twenty shillings, the Doctor went into the cellar to examine his recent purchase. The body was dead all right, dead drunk. It was the body of the village ale-can. He raced up the cellar steps and called after the rogues that the body was not dead. They shouted

Bradfield Watch House - note the sheep keeping the graveyard tidy!

Mottram Church

back, *"Well, kill it."* The next night, the 'body' shared the fee with his pals in yet another drunken spree.

Bodysnatchers often called at the Chequers Inn, Froggatt Edge, when conveying corpses to Padley Woods either to hide until the coast was clear or to leave for the ants to strip the flesh from the bones to provide a clean skeleton. On one occasion a doctor and his servant called at the Chequers travelling by horse and trap. They left a third passenger, apparently an elderly female, huddled in the seat of the vehicle. The ostler at the Chequers was an interfering busybody who tried vainly to engage the old lady in conversation. After remarking upon the weather and other topics of general conversation he decided she must be dozing and gave her a gentle nudge which caused her to slump helplessly forward. He was horrified to see the features of a corpse exposed and without further investigation, took to his heels. It was several days later before he plucked up sufficient courage to return to work.

On another such occasion, a passenger was left propped up in a trap outside the Chequers while two resurrection men called for refreshment; after all digging up corpses as quickly and quietly as possible was thirsty work. Several locals suspecting that the callers were on their way to Padley Woods, decided to play a joke on them and they removed the corpse while one of them climbed into the trap in its place.

When the resurrectionists resumed their journey, one of them grasped the hand of the 'corpse' to prevent it from lurching forward as the trap swayed. With a gasp of horror, he exclaimed, *"Why, it's warm!"*

"Yes, and so would you be if you'd been where I have," was the sepulchral reply.

The two were so terrified that they leapt from the trap and disappeared down the road at top speed. The abandoned horse and trap were never claimed and were later sold by the jokers who divided the proceeds between them.

'The Resurrectionist' was the title given to an unpublished article of William Wood's 'Tales and Traditions of the Peak', and the author explains the reason for its withdrawal in the preface. "One of the tales in the prospectus, 'The Resurrectionist', I have omitted as some of the details might not accord with the feelings of many at the present time." The work must have contained references to practitioners of the trade who were still very much alive and who would certainly not welcome publicity. As the resurrectionists were capable of any violence in the pursuit of their trade it was probably a wise precaution at the time, but it is a pity that he did not leave us the details.

This lost story of William Wood's is a reminder of the heat that is generated when anyone is so bold as to mention the former business of the manufacture of 'Dog Fat'. The practitioners of this trade would collect any stray dogs, fatten them up and later slaughter them and rend their bodies down for the fat. The stench which this process produced was absolutely shocking by all accounts, but the final product was held to work wonders for aches and pains on account of its remarkably penetrative properties.

Old men swore that it could penetrate a granite set overnight. Whenever the practice has been mentioned in recent years there have been letters to the local press from outraged relatives denying that their antecedents had anything to do with making dog fat. Despite these protestations of innocence, just about any old person can point to the very house where it took place.

Bodysnatching gradually came to an end after a Bill was passed through Parliament in 1832; this provided for the bodies of men and women who died in hospitals and workhouses, and were not claimed within 72 hours, to be sold for dissection. This assured the surgeons of a supply of bodies at a much lower price and the trade in stolen bodies died away immediately.

However that did not mean that everything was satisfactory in the burial business as the following letter from a dissatisfied citizen illustrates:

Funerals at Tideswell Church. 6.2.1875

Sir - Pardon me for these few observations. One day last week in passing through Tideswell I called to inspect the works that are being done to renovate the Parish Church. During my walk through the churchyard I was sensibly struck with an offensive smell through which my attention was drawn to a grave that had been made. At the bottom was a coffin visible enough to be seen and on the earth at the top was laid the bones of a person.

I do not know if such an act of burial is customary in that churchyard, viz., to take up one corpse to relay another, or if such is done with the consent of the Vicar. But in order that attention should be drawn to the fact and that the atmosphere is not diluted with pestilence and the fever raging, I ask you sir, to insert these facts,

I remain - Your faithful servant. A Traveller

Law and Order

At a time when swindlers, vandals, felons and lawbreakers in general, tremble in terror at the thought of being condemned to a period of community service, it might be opportune to take a look at the way malefactors were dealt with in the past.

The Anglo-Saxons introduced their own customs, laws and language much of which remains with us to this day. During the Anglo-Saxon period Townships were formed, consisting of ten or more families; the area was defined, as a rule, by natural borders, such as streams or peculiar landmarks, and their boundaries can generally be traced to the present day. Each township was responsible for the good behaviour of its inhabitants and, since in the event of any crime or damage being committed by one of its members, the loss had to be made good by the whole community, it naturally resulted in everyone being practically special constables. This system of collective responsibility was known as Frankpledge. Crimes in those days were mainly punished by a series of fines, even murder being commuted by a fine.

Later the Townships were run by the Lord of the Manor's Court Leet and the Vestry Meeting consisting of the Vicar, Churchwardens, and the Constable. Two hundred years ago the only persons exempt from serving in the office of Churchwarden were Peers of the Realm, Members of Parliament, lawyers, clergymen, dissenters, felons, and militia men. They were chosen at Easter by the joint consent of the minister and parishioners; if not, then one by the minister and the other by the parishioners. Refusal to accept the office could be punished by ex-communication. The oath was: *"You shall swear truthfully and faithfully to execute the office of churchwarden within your parish, and according to the best of your skill and knowledge present such things and persons as to your knowledge are presentable by the laws ecclesiastical of this realm; so help you God, and the contents of this book."*

By this oath they are empowered to sue for the goods of the church, bring an action of trespass for them and purchase goods for the use of the parish. They could levy a church rate by calling a vestry meeting, of which due notice had to be given, if the majority at the meeting empowered them to do so. Ratepayers only had the right or power to vote. The Church Rate was for the expenses of keeping the Church in repair. The rates for the repair of the Church shall be laid upon every occupier of lands in the parish, although such occupiers live in another parish.

Churchwardens and constables had many duties and powers: they were overseers of the poor; they could levy a fine of 12d on persons not attending Church on Sunday; they could levy a penalty of 3s 4d for practising unlawful sports on the Lord's Day; they could receive penalties from persons gaming in public houses, tippling and drunkenness, hawking spirituous liquors. In addition they could levy penalties relating to weights and measures and hawkers and pedlars trading without a licence had to be carried before a Justice of the Peace.

The members of the Vestry were particularly concerned to keep the costs of the Township to a minimum. Fathers who deserted their wives and children, and fathers of illegitimate children were pursued and made to pay for their upkeep as otherwise the expense would have to be borne by the Township. Rewards could be offered for information leading to the apprehension of the defaulters. Men who refused to work to support their families could be taken before a J.P. and sentenced to a spell on the treadmill if they did not start work straight away.

Overseers of Parishes were first appointed by Act of Parliament in 1601, and overseers of townships in 1633. Many Acts of Parliament have been passed to regulate dealing with the poor; by Acts of Parliament passed in 1349 no one was allowed to give to a beggar able to work; in 1388 the poor had to reside in the place where they were born and depend on the charity of those who knew them; in 1391 appropriators were obliged to give annually a sum for the support of the poor; in 1495 the poor were allowed to beg in the Hundred in which they resided; in 1530 every able-bodied man caught begging was taken and publicly whipped; in 1536 a systematic attempt was made to relieve the poor who were in great distress owing to the dissolution of the monasteries and monastic establishments; in 1601 overseers were ordered to erect poorhouses and given power to levy Poor Rates on householders.

In 1834 the numerous and ancient Poor Law Acts were consolidated and Boards of Guardians instituted. The country made no allowance for the keep of the inmates; they had to work or starve, and the Master had the power to flog them and put them in irons if he so thought fit. It was the reports of the treatment dealt out to inmates of these workhouses that gave the feeling of dread of entering one, and the Poor House and the Workhouse became as one in the minds of the people. The Poor Law was administered in a harsh manner by Boards of Guardians to deter people from entering and to cause people to leave them. In the 1870s the Board of Guardians at Glossop purchased a cartload of meal for thirty shillings and with it made a nourishing broth to be distributed to the inmates daily in winter. The scheme had to abandoned within a few weeks because the word of this bonanza spread far and wide and the Workhouse was overwhelmed with vagrants who travelled for miles in the hope of a bowlful of broth.

The Court Leet, Constables and Prisons

In addition to the Vicar, Churchwardens and Constables running the Township on a day to day basis, there was also the Court Leet. This is an ancient court dating from Anglo-Saxon times, but the institution of County Courts with loss of much of the Court Leets' authority and jurisdiction, has gradually led to most of the latter being abandoned.

Formerly the Lord of the Manor held Court Leets twice a year, at which the Constable or Headborough, the keeper of the stocks and pillory, the pound keeper, and other parochial officers were elected. At the opening of the Court Leet, the Lord of the Manor read the ancient address to those summoned to the Leet:-

"And I must tell you that these Leets and law days are very ancient laws, and they were the first laws that were used here in England; and they were ordained for two causes, the one was that the King might understand by his Steward upon the view of such persons as appeared before him how many men there were within the precincts of every law day to do service in his wars if need should require, for we must understand that at that time all Leets and law days were in the King's hand.

And at this day no man can keep a law day, but either by the King's special grant or else by title or which first began by the King's grant. And the cause was for the administration of Justice to the inhabitants within the precincts of every Leet or law day, for before the beginning of those Leets or law days there was no law user, no, nor no justice ministered, but all before the King himself; and wheresoever he was there was the law held and justice ministered, and in no place else.

And then by reason of the great number of suitors which resorted to the Court for law and justice, oftentimes sickness and diseases were brought thither, which did endanger the King's person; and also by reason of the multitude of suits which were there depending, it was long ere matters could be heard and determined, and very troublesome and chargeable to suitors to repair so far and stay so long for justice. For remedy thereof, this realm was then divided into counties, and so into hundreds, ridings, laths, leets, and wapentakes, which are all one in effect, though they may differ in name according to the custom of every county. And there is no man living within the realm but he is resident and abiding within the precinct of some one of these, and there he ought to appear twice every year, if he be not otherwise privileged by his place or office; and if any wrong be done unto any man under the value of forty shillings, then he ought to have redress, and not elsewhere."

At this Court disputes between tenants of the Manor were settled; the Court had power to deal with false measures, selling bad meat, smoky chimneys, privies in offensive condition, tippling in ale houses, bawdy houses, defects in bridges and highways, destroyers of ancient boundaries, bakers, brewers, curriers, eaves droppers, destroyers of game, hedge breakers, neglecters of hue and cry, inn holders, millers, night walkers, common nuisances, want of pillory and stocks and common pounds, scolds, shoemakers, searchers of leather, stoned horses of two years old put on the common, victuallers, constables neglecting watch and ward, weights and measures, and many others by particular statutes. The Court Leet could fine, but not imprison.

Dishonest tradesmen caught giving false measure or selling faulty goods could be fastened to a chair in front of their shop, hooted by the mob, and pelted with rotten eggs, dead cats and rats and other rubbish collected by small boys, or taken to a convenient pond and ducked. They were also liable to be nailed by an ear to their own doorpost or placed in the pillory and their rotten goods burned under their nostrils. Lords of the Manor claimed the right to erect their own pillory, and a pillory was considered so important that a village could lose its market if it did not have one.

The stocks were in use from Anglo-Saxon times and were used to secure offenders awaiting trial as well as being employed to humiliate criminals in a similar manner to the pillory. By a Statute of 1405, a village without a set of stocks could be downgraded to a mere hamlet, and by another Statute of 1426 beggars were ordered to be locked in the stocks for three days and nights on bread and water and then expelled from the township. There are still plenty of stocks and Stocks Lanes scattered about the Peak, in Eyam, Wormhill, Wardlow, Mottram, and Chapel-en-le Frith for example.

Heretics were burned quicke (alive), as were women who poisoned their husbands, while a male poisoner was sentenced to be boiled to death in water or lead.

Boiling to death was abolished in 1547. Many offences were punished by cutting off one or both ears and if a persistent criminal had no ears, then he could be branded on the cheek. Sheep stealers had their hands cut off; there was no concern about humiliating the criminal.

The office of Head or Chief Constable dates from 1285, the time of Edward I and is the office of the chief conservator of the peace in the county. Petty constable is the conservator of the peace in the hamlet or village, chief constable the head of the police in a city or borough. The village constable's duties were many, and it was a responsible office; if there was no one willing to undertake the duty, then it was compulsory upon those who occupied the land, and they had to take the office in rotation. The Constable had to execute all warrants issued by a Justice of the Peace, convey to the stocks anyone committing a breach of the peace and keep him there until he could convey him to gaol or safer custody. The prisoner was liable to pay all of his and the Constables expenses; if he had no money, distraint was made upon his goods; if he had no goods, then the Overseers had to find the Constable's expenses out of the Poor Rates. The Constable was also responsible for the building, repairing and surveying of bridges.

Every able bodied householder was liable to be sworn in as a Special Constable. For many years the custom of appointing Special Constables has been in abeyance. At one time, Special Constables' staffs could be seen in many houses, tied with ribbon and decorating the wall of a room. They were generally purchased by the friends of the person appointed, and often were presented at a little supper held at the favourite hostelry of the recipient, but the ordinary staffs were provided out of the poor rates. By law these staves should be returned at the termination of the office, but the staves were often kept as mementos of their period of office. In the 1940s my grandmother kept to hand in a drawer beside her armchair the staff which had been issued to her grandfather a hundred years earlier.

The punishment meted out for being found guilty of a crime varied considerably. Those who could show proof of literacy by reading the 51st Psalm could claim 'benefit of clergy' which was a measure intended to protect clergymen who could be tried in a secular court. This psalm became known appropriately as the 'neck verse'. William the Conqueror banned the death penalty, not because of any moral scruples, but because he wanted every available man to serve in his army. Under later kings this policy changed until by the time of George III there were over 200 capital crimes on the statute books. In 1823 the number was halved and from then onwards the number of capital offences was steadily reduced. Pressing to death, hanging for cattle, horse and sheep stealing and house breaking, were all abolished during this period, as was dissection after hanging.

Depending on the judge, the fate of a criminal could be a lottery, even children being hanged for petty theft, the decision sometimes hanging on the jury's opinion of the value of the stolen goods. If valued at one shilling or more the accused could face the gallows, but if the jury decided that they were only worth eleven pence then he might escape with a relatively light punishment. Throughout the ages, the wealthy have often been able to buy their way out of trouble, either by engaging the best lawyers or by paying a substantial fine.

In 1705 John Crossland and his two sons were convicted of horse stealing at Bakewell, and after sentence was passed, the bench offered to pardon one, if he would hang the other two. This offer was first made to the father, who refused; then to the older son who also declined. The youngest son, John, accepted and hung his father and brother without remorse. Afterwards he was employed as the hangman for Derbyshire and neighbouring counties until he was too old to continue in that grim office.

Criminals were not the only ones to suffer at the hands of the law. Anyone whose religious beliefs did not meet with the approval of the government of the day could find it a very expensive, or even fatal business. Failure to attend at the designated place of worship could lead to heavy fines, which was one of the main reasons for pursuing the recusants. Some got round this problem by attending their own place of worship secretly and openly attending the Parish Church later. In Manor Park Glossop, in a corner of the Rose Garden close to the bridge which leads to what was once Lord Howard's fish pond, there stood a small Chapel which Catholics attended before going to Old Glossop Church. As this was part of the grounds of the Howards they were fairly safe from interference. This little Chapel was swept away by the great flood of 1944.

The Peak was long an outpost of the old religion and hence a favourite refuge for Catholics hiding from persecution. Two Derbyshire priests, Nicholas Garlick and Robert Ludlam, were captured during a search of Padley Hall. After being held in Derby gaol they were condemned at the following assizes to to be hung drawn and quartered, which barbarous sentence was duly carried out.

One of the active pursuivants or recusant hunters employed by the Privy Council at this time was one Anthony Atkinson, of Hull. On October 24th 1593, he wrote to Cecil with respect to Derbyshire:

"And further some flee thee into Derbyshire into the hie peeke and there is one Robartt Eyre a justice of peace onely for that country and he favouringe his brother Robert Eyre and many of his Kynsmen who are recusants, gives warning when any search is portended and so makes them flee into the mountaynes in the peeke country where the papists have harbors in the every-peakes and there are relieved by sheppards, so that country is a sanctuary for all wycked men, and is more used of late than ever was in respect of the justices of peace, butt he hath now fellowes that are under the popes dyspensation, which may do anything to the ayd of papists, eyther go to the church or be in authority or obey any commandments upon safeguard of life, landes, or goodes."

It was during these times that wealthy landlords who held to Roman Catholicism had priest holes built into some of their properties. Lees Hall in Simmondley was rumoured to have a priest hole, but Lord Howard would not allow a search to be made while he owned the property. Perhaps he thought it might be needed again one day! During the 1960s when structural alterations were being made, the hideaway was discovered and found to contain a bed which had once hung from the wall by chains, a three-legged stool and a roll of documents. From the reports of the constables we find that in 1643 there were 158 recognised recusants in the High Peak out of a total of 313 in the whole county.

Following a statute transportation was introduced in the reign of George I in 1718, and many criminals were transported to America. Between 1718 and the time when the American penal settlements were closed as a result of the American War of Independence, 199 prisoners were sent from Derbyshire. The court appointed specific judges who were responsible for arranging the transportation of the criminals. The judge communicated with a contractor, whose job it was to transport the criminal to America. The court on average gave him between 2 and 3 guineas for the service. The contractor had the personal property of the criminal for this, and in America sold him to the highest bidder. Naturally the whole process was legalised with papers.

When prisoners could not be transported to America anymore, a new penal settlement was established in 1787 at Botany Bay, New South Wales. In 1840 the settlement was transferred to Tasmania. Between the years 1787 and 1857, when transportation was abolished, 108,715 convicts were transported from Britain. There is a popular notion that they were all sent for stealing a loaf of bread. Some were certainly petty criminals, but many were utter scoundrels lucky to escape the gallows; yet others were what today would be called political prisoners having been involved in forming Trade Unions, or machine breaking, or even denouncing the government of the day.

The work of administering the law was left to the gentry of the county. Wealthy landowners were chosen by the state and given the title of Justice of the Peace and allowed to get on with the job. They were unpaid for their work, but were empowered to levy rates because, although the system was intended to be run as cheaply as possible, there were inevitable expenses in managing prisons, escorting prisoners, and payments for clerical work. In addition to administering the law, the JPs were responsible for seeing that roads and bridges were kept in a state of good repair, and licensing of taverns and other tasks which today would be carried out by Councils. JPs sat often in pairs in Courts of Petty Sessions in the major towns to hand out justice to poachers, beggars, drunkards and thieves. Being landowners they could hardly be expected to deal with poachers in an even handed fashion. Later with the growth of the cotton industry, many of the mill owners became the wealthiest in the district and in due course became JPs.

So long as the High Peak was an agricultural district, the police system was quite sufficient to keep order, but with the advent of strangers coming to work in the cotton mills and the consequent increase of crime, the voluntary system broke down and eventually a County Police Force was set up. An Act was passed in 1839 which allowed the counties to establish their own police forces along the lines of the London police. Many counties took advantage of the Act but Derbyshire was among those counties which waited until 1856 when a further Act compelled each county to establish a regular force.

When the original Act was passed the Derbyshire JPs appointed a committee to consider the formation of a local force and to sound out public opinion on the matter. There were plenty of objections, mainly on the grounds of cost, but among other reasons given were that there was no need for such a body because there was little or no crime in their locality which could not easily be dealt with by the existing system of parish constables. Another real and well justified fear was that the new police might come to have a political role and be engaged in spying on the public in the government interest as was common on the continent. This is why police forces in Britain were run by local watch committees and why there has been concern every time forces have been amalgamated in the name of efficiency or used for political ends as during strikes.

One argument used in support of a county force was that if one was not formed and the neighbouring counties did, then the thieves, beggars and rogues would all move into Derbyshire for easy pickings. In an effort to keep costs to a minimum the JPs committee recommended that Derbyshire should have a force of sixty constables with six superintendents and a chief Constable. This was one third the number permitted by Act of Parliament.

The earliest prison recorded in the High Peak was at Bakewell in the year 1286. In 1588, the newly built prison for the County of Derby was opened. It was notorious amongst the prisoners, even in such harsh times, for its foulness and resulting frequent visitations from the plague and gaol fever. If the authorities had been determined to economise on the cost of keeping prisoners by siting the prison where fatal disease was a virtual certainty they could hardly have found a better spot. The prison was built in the Corn Market over an open brook, in those days an open sewer. If this was not bad enough, in the year 1610, the brook rose suddenly in the night and drowned three of the prisoners before they could be rescued from their cells.

Elizabethan legislation provided that in every shire there should be at least one House of Correction for rogues, vagabonds and sturdy beggars. During the reign of James I this legislation was more specifically defined; in addition to there being places of detention for rogues, vagabonds, and those who by incorrigible and dangerous habits set the local constable at defiance, all such poor persons as would not employ themselves on appointed work were therein to be imprisoned. The shires were ordered to provide their houses with *"convenient backsides thereto adjoining together with mills, turns, cards and suchlike necessary employment to set the rogues and other idle persons on".*

There were three of these Houses of Correction in the Peak, at Tideswell, Wirksworth and Ashbourne. The House of Correction at Tideswell was established in

Chapel-en-le-Frith Stocks

Eyam Stocks

Lees Hall, once moated, had a priest hole.

1711 with William Shore as keeper at an annual salary of £20. The cell measured only 6' 6" by 5' 7" but in 1741 it had to hold as many as twenty vagrants in a single night because the prison at Chesterfield had been closed by the justices who objected to being sent consignments of vagrants from Nottinghamshire. Smaller villages often had small lock-ups, or round houses used to confine local drunks and vagrants. Most have disappeared or been turned into cottages, but there is one in Market Street, Hayfield, built in 1799. Beside it is a small square, named appropriately Dungeon Row.

The authorities did not like the notion of prisoners passing their time in idleness, as they might use such spare time to educate one another further in the ways of villainy. To keep them hard at work the treadmill was introduced in 1817. It could accommodate up to twenty four men standing almost shoulder to shoulder, the men being separated by partitions so they could not see or converse with their neighbours. The treadmill had twenty four 8 inch steps and the prisoners toiled away trying to climb the steps which moved away from under them. To prevent them falling under the device and being crushed, they held onto a rail. All the energy produced was put to no useful purpose other than exhausting the prisoners who referred to the exercise as grinding air. This did not deter the authorities as it was intended to grind rogues honest.

Another contrivance which occupied prisoners in useless toil was the crank. This machine consisted of a drum with a long handle at one end. Turning the handle caused cups inside to scoop up sand from the bottom of the drum which fell out of the cups once they reached the top of a revolution. The number of revolutions was recorded on a dial and the prisoner had to turn away steadily until 1000 revolutions had been completed, the prisoner receiving no food until he had achieved this total.

Among the duties of the master of these prisons named in the Orders of 1719 was the whipping of prisoners. A sheep stealer was ordered by the justices to be whipped in open market at Ashbourne in the forenoon, and at Dovebridge in the afternoon; and for quelling any disturbance that might be attempted by his relatives and confederates, the keeper of the Ashbourne House of Correction was to take the late Act of Parliament for quelling riots and to publicly read it before each flogging.

In 1708 Cuthbert Rodgerson and Mary his wife were both found guilty of Petty Larceny. It was "*Ordered both be whipped through the market in the height thereof, to be stripped to the waist and whipped at a carts ars from one end of the town of Wirksworth unto the other.*" Later in the 18th century malefactors were sentenced to be whipped privately inside the gaol instead of publicly in the Market Place.

All these public duties had to be paid for and in the records of the County Treasurer for 1782-83 the following items appear:-

To Mr Simpson, gaol fees, and whipping prisoners	£ 1- 3s - 4d
To Mr Simpson for taking two prisoners to be transported	£11- 0s- 0d
To Mr Simpson, year's straw for the felons..................	£ 8- 8s- 0d

Gaoler's Salary 1775: *It is ordered by this Court that the sum of twenty pounds be raised and paid by the Treasurer of this County to Blyth Simpson, Keeper of His Majesty's Gaol for this County in discharge of one year's salary for executing that office ending Michaelmas last.*

Dated 1774; *Elizabeth Webster - a vagabond in the custody of the Master of the House of Correction at Chesterfield by Warrant under the Hand and Seal of Brabazon Hallows esq. one of His Majesty's Justices of the Peace for this County and being brought before this Court -- This Court doth order that the said Elizabeth Webster be privately whipped by the said Master of the House of Correction and be then taken by him as soon as conveniently may be to some of his Majesty's Justices of the Peace acting for this County to be sent to the place of her last legal settlement.*

The King v Jane Archer 1775: *Jane Archer late of the Parish of Wirksworth in the County of Derby singlewoman being indicted arraigned and tried for feloniously stealing, taking and carrying away one Woman's Silk Hat and one Silk Handerkerchief to the value of one shilling of the goods and chattels of one John Sumers and being found guilty thereof. It is ordered by this Court that the said Jane Archer be committed into the custody of Blyth Simpson Keeper of His Majesty's Gaol for this County for the space of one month and then to be privately whipped and discharged out of custody.*

Gallows and Gibbets

Scattered throughout England are grim reminders of the past, perpetuated in such place names as Gallows Clough, Gibbet Moor and Gallows Moss.

Although gibbeting was not a legal part of the sentence until 1752, when the judges were empowered to order either that the body of the criminal should be hung in chains, or that it should be given to the surgeons for dissection, there are earlier instances of gibbeting within the county of Derby. In 1341, the bodies of three men executed for highway robbery with violence were hung in chains outside Chapel-en-le-Frith. During the same year a woman and two men were dealt with in the same way on Ashover Moor for murdering the King's Purveyor. During the time of the Commonwealth there are two further references to cases of gibbeting, one was on Sinfin Moor and the other near Wirksworth. The site of this is still known locally as 'Gibbet Knoll' and stands on the high ground to the west of the town. The spot is not marked on the map, but we must not be too hard on the surveyors since they rely on locals in the first instance for their information and having gleaned the facts they then have to decide what to include and what to omit. The early surveyors must have had an interesting time trying to decipher the local dialect, it can be hard enough today for a stranger enquiring the way.

After a hanging, the body of the executed criminal was taken down and carried away in a cart to the County Hall for dissection or to be hung in chains on the gibbet until the crows pecked the flesh from his bones. When it was intended to hang the body from the gibbet it was the custom to measure the criminal for his 'last suit' of chains shortly before he was conveyed by cart to the gallows. Corpses were sometimes hacked down from the gallows by relatives in the hope of revival, and to keep the body from the clutches of the surgeons or the indignity of the gibbet. The word gibbet was originally synonymous with a gallows but later came to signify an upright post with a projecting arm from which the bodies of executed criminals were suspended.

Dr Clegg, the Non-Conformist minister of Chapel-en-le-Frith has left us a description of the grim ritual under the date August 31st 1731:

"Going to Ashford my way thither lay near Leek, and this being the day appointed for the execution of Nadin I went along that way. We met him on the common the gibbet was erected on. The Sheriff, whom I know, came first with his men, then the clergyman that had assisted the criminal, then the man carried the irons he was to hang in, then came the prisoner, then the gaoler, and lastly the hangman. The curate of Leek spent an hour in praying and exhorting him, then the 51st Psalm was sung, and after some time the executioner did his office."

It was the practice to saturate the body with tar before it was hung in chains in order that it might hang there for a long period as an example to others. This was done with the bodies of three highwaymen gibbeted on the top of the Chevin near Belper. After they had been hanging for a few weeks, the gibbet which bore all three was set alight by a friend of the criminals. Nearby villagers, seeing the glare, climbed the hill to be met with the ghastly sight of the three bodies blazing in the darkness. By morning, only the chains remained on the site.

The last gibbet in England is reputed to have stood on the green at Wardlow Mires. Alas, in this matter, local tradition is wrong; the last man to be gibbeted in England was a bookbinder named James Cook executed for murder. On 1st August 1832 he was suspended in iron hoops. A little earlier in the same year, James Cox was hung up at Aylestone near Leicester on a gibbet 30 feet high. This caused such disturbances by sightseers on Sundays and Holidays that the Home Office ordered the body to be buried. Gibbeting was abolished in 1834.

On New Year's Day, 1815, Anthony Lingard of Tideswell murdered a toll-keeper, Mrs Hannah Oliver, at Wardlow Mires. This inhuman wretch strangled the old woman with a handkerchief and tried to make it look as if she had taken her own life. She was killed because Lingard wanted her new pair of red shoes; he also stole a sum of money. The murderer offered the shoes and money to a young woman who was pregnant by him with a view to inducing her to father the child on some other man. The young woman suspecting the shoes to be stolen refused to accept them so Lingard hid them in a haystack, later recovered them and stupidly concealed them in his home where they were found by those investigating the crime.

The shoes had been made for Mrs Oliver by Samuel Marsden, a shoemaker of Stoney Middleton and he was to prove a crucial witness at Lingard's trial. In an age when shoes were made by hand it was a straightforward matter for a tradesman to recognise his own work and Samuel Marsden had no hesitation in declaring the shoes to have been made by him. To remove any possible doubt as to the identification he offered to take one to pieces because he remembered using a piece of packing in the heel which bore the inscription "Commit no crime." When the heel was opened the evidence was revealed and Lingard's guilt established.

Anthony Lingard was hanged at Derby on 8th March 1815 and his body brought to Wardlow to hang in chains near the scene of his crime as an example to all. When his body was being conveyed to Wardlow an unusual incident is reputed to have occurred. When the soldiers forming the escort reached Rowsley they marched on through Beeley instead of turning left towards Bakewell and in due course entered the private grounds of Chatsworth House where they were told they could proceed no further by one of the Duke's servants. "Duke he may be," replied the young officer in charge, "but I hold the King's Commission. Quick march." and the grim procession carried on its way. The upshot of this incident was that the road was no longer private under an ancient law whereby the passage of a corpse along a road made it a public right of way.

Once at Wardlow, tradesmen of all sorts set up stalls to cater for the huge crowds who flocked around the gruesome spectacle. Tumblers and entertainers performed and pickpockets had a field day among the spectators.

Mr Longden, who lived at Upper House Farm in the Woodlands and later became landlord of the Snake Inn, and who was also a Methodist Minister, went to Tideswell to preach on that day, but found no sign of the congregation. Enquiries soon revealed that they had all decamped to Wardlow to see the gibbeting. A man not easily put off, he followed his flock and addressed them from under the very gibbet, using the shocking sight to emphasise the message of his sermon.

The efficacy of the gibbet as a deterrent is called into question by the fact that Anthony Lingard's brother William was sentenced 11 years later for highway robbery and assault, and was reprieved. The robbery was committed within view of the gibbet on which the bleached bones of his brother were hanging.

Lingard's body remained suspended for several years and the new toll keepers could hear the skeleton rattle in its frame as wintry gales howled across the dreary moors around Wardlow. This gibbet was taken down on April 20th 1826 and Lingard's remains buried on the site. Several relics of the crime were preserved including the warrant for Lingard's arrest, the handcuffs he wore when captured and the shoe-makers rule used to make the shoes which proved his guilt. A beam from the gibbet was used in the construction of a cottage cellar and several stones previously used as supports were used in building a barn at Wardlow Mires. Another gruesome relic was a toasting fork made from the frame which held the rotting corpse. Lingard's skull was subsequently taken to Belle Vue, presumably as an exhibit.

The cost of apprehending Anthony Lingard was £31 5s 5d; and the cost of the gibbeting £53 18s 8d. In addition there was the fee of 10 guineas paid to the gaoler for conveying the body from Derby to Wardlow.

There are several aspects of this grisly tale which would stand further investigation. The inscription on the packing used in the shoe heel has all the hallmarks of a Victorian melodrama where the sins of the sinner seek him out. The Snake Inn was known as Lady Clough House until 1824 and members of the Longden family were tenants there until 1879. Several of them are buried in the churchyard at Hope. No inn comparable to the present Snake Inn would have existed before the opening of the road in 1821, since the only travellers would have been packhorse men, badgers, drovers, and the occasional horseman. John Longden could not have been the landlord at the Snake Inn in 1815 several years before it was built to cater for travellers on Thomas Telford's new turnpike road. The incident when the body was taken through Chatsworth has probably been improved with the telling; the gaoler certainly would not want to spend too much of his ten guineas on a military escort.

Wardlow Mires may not be able to claim the site of the last gibbet in England but Gibbet Moor to the east of Chatsworth House did not gain that grim name without a cause. One day a woman was frying some bacon in her cottage by the moorside when a tramp came to her door. He asked for food but she replied that she had nothing for him. When he pointed to the frying pan she retorted that she was not cooking bacon for such an idler as himself. The ruffian attacked her, knocking her to the ground and in a rage poured the boiling fat from the pan down her throat thus scalding her to death.

Her murderer was sentenced to be hanged alive in chains by the cottage door where his victim had lived and the gibbet was set up on the very spot. He was a long time in dying and his screams as he swung in the wind were so piercing that they disturbed the peace of the noble resident of Chatsworth over the hill. He was so haunted by the ghastly occurrence that he took steps to have the terrible practice abolished and it is claimed that this was the last occasion that a man was gibbeted alive in England.

Some strange superstitions were once attached to gallows and gibbets. A dead man's hand was supposed to have the quality of dispelling tumours or swollen glands by striking with it nine times the place affected. After the criminal had been hanging several minutes people suffering from these afflictions would approach the gallows and the hangman, having untied the hanged man's hand would stroke the affected part several times with it. The hand of a person dying a violent death was deemed particularly efficacious and nurses would bring sick children to be stroked with the hands of executed criminals. A halter wherewith any one had been hanged, if tied about the head was guaranteed to cure a headache and many other cures. The chips or cutting from a gibbet or gallows, on which one or more persons had been executed or exposed, if worn next the skin, or round the neck in a bag, would cure the ague or prevent it. The executioner, of course, could earn himself a useful income by performing such services.

Public Disorder

Where the government of the day refuses to listen to the wishes and aspirations of common people as so frequently happens, in the end public disorder becomes the only recourse. Perhaps the barons who forced King John to sign Magna Carta at Runnymede in 1215 started the ball rolling. They were only concerned with their own rights and never gave a thought to other classes, but if they could claim rights why not any other group? From the Peasants' Revolt of 1381 which was the result of a third Poll Tax, to the recent uproar over the attempted introduction of an absurd tax of the same name, a determined refusal to listen has been manifest. In nearly every case the outcome is the same; the ringleaders are denounced and often dealt with severely, but the tax or other cause for anger is eventually quietly quashed.

There have been Militia riots, Reform Bill and Chartist riots in an effort to extend the franchise; Luddite riots to protect employment; Turnpike riots often provoked by local small businessmen; but most common of all, food riots in time of scarcity. Not all these disturbances were concerned with popular demands for rights and liberties, some in large towns were deliberately started by criminals so that they could break into property, or pick pockets during the riot. However, in general it is difficult to provoke such behaviour without some underlying cause.

Food riots were virtually certain to occur after years of poor harvest. As bread was the staple diet of the working population, any decrease in the supply and resulting increase cost of bread soon led to discontent. Wheaten bread was the most common form in lowland areas, but certainly in the upland parishes of the Peak, folks had to subsist on oaten bread. After a poor harvest, prices could rise very rapidly indeed; in 1795, for instance, wheat prices rose from 57 shillings a quarter in January to 111 shillings by July. In the period 1799-1803 prices soared from 53 shillings a quarter in June 1799 to 146 shillings by February 1801, eventually reaching 152 shillings a quarter by February 1803. As if this was not bad enough, many were thrown out of work because so much of their income was spent on bread that there was nothing to spare for manufactured goods. Thus the ideal conditions for a riot were created; unemployment and consequent poverty coinciding with bread prices beyond the means of most.

Dealers were a target for popular discontent since they were seen as profiting from the shortages. If, for example, it became known that a dealer was intending to sell local grown grain in another area where he could obtain a better price, it was not unknown for a mob to stop the wagons and force them to return to the home region. In the event of refusal, the wagons would be emptied and their contents distributed among the crowd.

Another likely to incur the wrath of the populace was the miller who was relatively free to charge his own price for grinding corn for the poor and was also able to increase his profits by mixing inferior grain with that of his customers. Millers had a reputation for defrauding their customers which went back for centuries. In the Prologue of Chaucer's 'Canterbury Tales' we are treated to a description of just such a rogue.

> "He was a master-hand at stealing grain
> He felt it with his thumb and thus he knew
> Its quality and took three times his due -
> A thumb of gold, by God, to gauge an oat"

The following extract comes from the Manchester Guardian 27th August 1825, which suggests that such malpractices were still occurring at that time:

To Detect Adulterated Flour:- Take a teaspoonful of flour, putting it in a wine glass, which fill up with clean water, stirring it up well; allow it to stand for half an hour, then decant the milky fluid off the top, which consists of a starch in a state of solution. To the remainder add a teaspoonful of sulphuric acid, which if it is pure will dissolve the whole of it; allow it to remain for ten minutes, then fill the glass again with water, when the burnt bones, plaster of Paris, or chalk, will easily be discovered at the bottom. Should the adulteration consist of chalk, a violent effervescence will ensue upon the addition of the acid.

Or take a small quantity of the suspected flour, put it on an iron spoon, pass the flame of a candle with a blow pipe upon it. Should it be pure, it will turn black; but if it contains any of the above mentioned ingredients, the white particles will immediately be visible.

In September 1756 at Wirksworth *'a great mob arose, and pulled down several Corn Mills in that neighbourhood'*. A week later mills in the town and neighbourhood of Derby were attacked by 'a large numbers of Miners, and other persons out of the Peak.' The principal grievance for destroying the mills was the use by certain millers of 'French Burr stones' in the grinding of corn. These were held to work against the interests of the poor because the newly arrived French millstones ground the flour finer than the local Peak stones and made easier the adulteration of the grain. Millers were accused of grinding peas and beans, and even lime and plaster. One miller was well known to boast that he could grind ten pounds of grain into twenty pounds of flour.

This destruction of mills was clearly well organised because the rioters gave prior warning of their intention of destroying only those mills using French stones and proceeded to do exactly that. Mills which used the local millstones were untouched, as were those who promptly disposed of the offending French stones. The import of the

French grindstones also ruined the trade of manufacturing stones locally which no doubt accounts for the 'other persons out of the Peak' marching down to destroy them. Some idea of the former importance of the grindstone trade can be gleaned by looking at the hundreds of finished stones lying below Stanage and Millstone Edges above Hathersage.

This form of riot suggests that the crowd were concerned to impose the corn economy of the poor onto farmers, millers and dealers, which meant that prices should be regulated according to the means of the poor. In addition to destroying Corn Mills another way of controlling prices was for a huge mob to march onto the market of one of the larger towns, take what corn they wanted and pay what they considered to be a fair price. The typical Derbyshire rioters were the lead miners; living and working closely together in some numbers they had a unity and discipline not often found in agricultural workers. This discipline was invaluable for when they set out for bread they marched under captains and when forced to retire by the military they took refuge from their pursuers in the pits. It is one thing to cut down a man with a sabre when riding on horseback, but a very different matter to follow him into a lead mine on foot where your quarry might be waiting with a pickaxe on ground of his own choosing.

Food riots posed a difficult problem for the courts since they were caused by desperation rather than any political or criminal cause. If the courts were partial to the dealers, or severe in dealing with the rioters, they could easily precipitate even worse riots since those who took food and paid what they considered was a just price felt they had right on their side.

Dark Deeds in Chinley

A stranger passing through the scattered Township of Chinley, with its numerous farmsteads and cottages and quiet aspect, would never dream that its lonely lanes were once the haunt of thieves of the most audacious character. In the year 1844, in the month of July, in the solitary hours of night, a burglary of the most daring description was committed at a lonely farmhouse. The facts read like the actions of some aspiring followers of 'Jack Sheppard'. The farmhouse selected by the villains was Lower Ashen Clough, in Back Chinley on the road leading from Belle Vue, Chinley to Hayfield. Mr James Bennett, his wife, and a daughter were all in bed when the thieves struck.

There were three brothers called Swann from Ashton and Stalybridge comprising the gang, aged 21, 23, and 25 years respectively. They had evidently prepared themselves for the most desperate work, and came at dead of night armed, one with a pistol, one with a sword, and one with a stout cudgel. An impression seemed to have got abroad that as the estate had recently been sold, a large sum of money was concealed about the premises. The burglars had somehow got wind of this information. They gained access to the house by a window and upon finding little cash, they collected

Gateway to Lower Ashen Clough Farm.

every item of value such as spoons and knives. They then aroused the family, who were compelled by dire threats to remain in bed or give information as to the whereabouts of money and valuables. Here they were foiled and missed finding a sum of £20.

Not finding what they expected, the thieves made off with silk dresses, shawls, a gun and in fact anything they could carry away. Meantime the rascals made off towards Hayfield and Mellor. In the latter place they succeeded in breaking into another farmhouse and robbing an old woman of a few articles and money. The affair soon became noised abroad but almost all trace of the perpetrators had been lost except that their voices betrayed the neighbourhood from which they came.

To this day, local accents can change markedly in the distance of a few miles, so a hundred and fifty years ago it must have been fairly simple to place the origin of the thieves by their voices.

Justice was, however, hanging over their heads and they were suddenly arrested. Their downfall came about in the following fashion. A Mr Samuel Bennett caused a number of handbills to be circulated in Ashton, Stockport and other places describing the place, the articles stolen and offering a reward for their recovery. A Mr Glossop, brother of the Rev Glossop of Chinley Chapel, gained possession of one of these handbills in his travels and out of curiosity called at one or two pawnshops and found some of the articles pledged.

This information was conveyed to the Superintendents of Police in Ashton and

Stalybridge Boroughs, whose suspicions at once fell on the Swanns, who were known to the police as regular thieves. Police were thin on the ground in those days, so a degree of ingenuity was called for in making an arrest, but acting in concert the police provided themselves with the necessary apparatus to capture and carry off their men. One of the Superintendents who appeared to be on friendly terms with the Swanns made his way to their house. Here, the officer was invited to have a cup of tea and engaged them in conversation. Suddenly another officer burst in and pounced upon the trio and secured them after a furious struggle. The greatest confusion prevailed during the scuffle and the 'Wakes' dainties were scattered about the room.

The prisoners were at once conveyed in irons to the lock-up; much excitement being caused and a general feeling of relief experienced by tremulous housekeepers at the taking of such notorious scoundrels. A search of the sister's house fully justified their arrest. A large can full of pawn tickets was found. Large numbers of articles were recovered and plated vessels broken up to conceal their identity ready for melting down and sale. The sister referred to was wearing a gold ring which she had shown to companions a few days previously. It was marked inside with a peculiar mark and readily identified by Mrs Bennett of Chinley.

The whole family, including parents, were arrested and charged either with robbery, or receiving goods knowing them to have been stolen. After appearing before the Borough magistrates they were handed over to the Derbyshire Police and the whole ruffianly crew committed to the next Derbyshire Assizes. The judge commenting on their daring career sentenced all three brothers to penal servitude for life; their father to ten years; and the mother and daughter to three years between them.

Matlock Bridge: 17.10.1874

Delivering bread without weighing: William King, Baker, Matlock Bath, was charged with the above offence - P.C. Spencer stated that on the 6th inst. about half past four o'clock, he saw a lad in the employ of defendant delivering bread at certain houses from a cart in which there were no scales or weights. Defendant was fined 1 shilling and costs of 10s 6d.

Prize Fight at Harpur Hill. 23.5.1874

One morning early this week, a set fight, we understand for money, took place near Harpur Hill. Two men, employed, it is stated, at the Lime Works, were pitted against each other, and for half an hour did their best to injure each other. The termination was that one man, the smaller, had, to use a sporting term, "his peepers closed." This concluded the disgraceful scene. There were the usual scouts out to watch the police, who for the nonce were well looked after.

A Trip into Staffordshire

Some of the finest Peakland country lies in Staffordshire, so we are quite in order to make a sally across the River Dove and see what that county has to offer. The Roches and the Dane Valley are always worth a visit, but on the way from Buxton to Leek we pass close by the oddly named village of Flash. Flash lays claim to being the highest village in England at 1518 feet. In the past it earned a certain notoriety as a centre for the minting of 'spurious coin' and for the holding of pugilistic encounters, the three counties of Derbyshire, Cheshire and Staffordshire meeting at Three Shires Head about a mile away. The Postal Authorities may have long ago decided to change its name to Quarnford but the rest of us can, and must, go on calling it Flash.

How was this odd named derived? One explanation put forward is that the fabricators of counterfeit coin were called 'Flash men,' and the false coinage they produced was called Flash-money. Not very far away from Flash, a couple of miles to the north, is the Tinker's Pit at the convergence of the A537 and A54, yet another once quiet spot where the coiners plied their trade? Others hold that the etymology of Flash is derived from its situation, 'a bog, a marshy place.'

Being located close to the junction of three county boundaries the area was ideally situated for the brutal sport of prizefighting. Three Shires Head has seen plenty of such contests. On hearing that one of these affrays was to be staged in the locality, a Justice of the Peace went to see for himself what was afoot and found that the event was being held within his magisterial boundaries. Without a moments hesitation he ordered them off and the contestants obliged by stepping just across the county boundary. The J.P. and his party followed and watched the fight with keen interest, enjoying it so much that they contributed generously towards the subscriptions.

Moving down the valley of the Dane which forms the boundary between Staffordshire and Cheshire we pass by Gradbach where now stands a fine Youth Hostel which was previously a Silk Mill, and before that a Linen Mill. The mill went out of business when water power could no longer compete with the new fangled steam engines. Not far away from where the Black Brook joins the Dane stood Caster's Bridge which may have gained its name from the casting of metal nearby. This bridge was the scene of a narrow escape from a terrible fate in the distant past. At one time a brigand's hostel stood close by to which tired and lonely travellers were decoyed and murdered. In the days when there were thousands of itinerant workers moving about the country seeking work, if one of them disappeared without leaving a trace it is unlikely that anyone would have been the wiser. One night a weary pedlar sought a night's rest and he saw the robbers busily melting ore. Just as he was falling asleep he heard one of the children whisper the dread words, *"Mother, when will that queer old man be dead? I'm sure the oven is quite hot enough."* It seemed that not satisfied with murdering and robbing him, they intended to cook and eat him as well. The pedlar might have been tired and footsore but hearing these words he leapt to his feet and ran as fast as his legs

Staffordshire Peak Country. Gradbach and the Back Forest in the background.

Gradbach Mill on the River Dane was a large spinning mill. It is now a Youth Hostel and the old packhorse tracks that converge on it serve the many walking visitors to the area.

could carry him until he found a hiding place under the arch of Caster's Bridge. By this means he successfully eluded the murderous pack of men, women and dogs.

When at last they had given up the search the pedlar made his way to a nearby Staffordshire town where he gave evidence of his terrible experience before the authorities. A body of troops was immediately dispatched to surround the den which was then sacked and the desperadoes secured and escorted back to the town in chains where they were tried and hanged without delay.

Ludchurch

Here also is the ancient Back Forest of Swythamley which is said to have provided Robin Hood with yew for his bows, and high on the hillside, well hidden, is a natural cleft in the rocks known as Ludchurch. If you don't mind a stiff climb this is one of the finest stretches of walking country in the district with several well defined and sign-posted paths. The path to Ludchurch approaches by a zig-zag route since a direct approach would be like climbing a ladder. Were it not for the signposts it would be possible to miss it altogether.

The entrance to Ludchurch is by a narrow opening in the rock face and once inside the fissure widens into an impressive ravine whose sides are covered with mosses and ferns. I would estimate its dimensions to be 6-12 feet wide, 30-40 feet deep and perhaps more than a 100 yards long. It is easy to understand how such a well hidden and remote spot would be associated with secret meetings and legendary deeds.

Where does the name Ludchurch come from? One explanation given is that the name was derived from Ludd or Nudd, who was an ancient British god of the sun. According to tradition, his shrine was at Ludgate, an old London gate built in 66 BC.and named after him. There is also a tradition that an early British King was called Lud who was buried near Ludgate, and if you look at the paintings of English kings on the ceiling of Saint Mary's Church in Beverley you will find King Lud right at the end.

You will also discover tales of Ludchurch featuring such legendary figures as Robin Hood, Little John and Friar Tuck meeting there or Sir Gawain and the Green Knight, and more recently, part of the Pretender's army camping in its narrow confines in 1745 on their way to Derby. This is surely from the world of myth; the last time I visited Ludchurch was after a prolonged dry spell and it was still damp and muddy. Certainly not an ideal campsite when compared with the woodland around it.

If the previous stories belong to the realm of myth and legend, another tale connected with Ludchurch, that it was used by the Lollards as a meeting place, could have an historical basis. (The name Lollard was derived from the Dutch lollaert , meaning mumbler or hummer.) To learn more about this religious group we need to go back to the 14th century. John Wycliffe was born around 1330 in the North Riding of Yorkshire and was educated at Oxford. A theologian and church reformer, the promoter of the first complete translation of the Bible into English, he was one of the forerunners

Swythamley Forest.

Ludchurch.

of the Protestant Reformation. This first translation of the Bible was carried out by Nicholas of Hereford and later revised by Wycliffe's secretary, John Purvey. His theories required the church to give up its worldly possessions and in 1378 he began an attack on the beliefs and practices of the church. Naturally those in the established church living in some affluence responded in the usual manner of the privileged, but the Lollards propagated his controversial views. Ever since St Augustine converted the English to Christianity there had been an undercurrent of opposition to the idea of admitting the supremacy of a Pope based in Rome. William the Conqueror had difficulties in this connection, not being the type of king to admit to the supremacy of anyone. The question was, who was head of the church in England, the Pope or the reigning monarch? A contentious matter which came to the fore under Henry VIII.

In 1377 Parliament and the King consulted Wycliffe as to whether or not it was lawful to keep back treasure of the kingdom from Rome, and Wycliffe replied that it was. In May, Pope Gregory XI issued five bulls against him denouncing his theories and calling for his arrest so that he could be examined by leaders of the Roman Catholic Church. The call was ignored - Wycliffe had more sense than to go to Rome to defend his views. Oxford University refused to condemn its scholar and Wycliffe lived until December 1384 when he died as the result of a stroke.

In 1415 the Council of Constance decreed that Wycliffe's books be burned and his body exhumed. The books were burnt straight away but it was 13 years later that his body was disinterred, burned to ashes and scattered into the River Swift. The first Lollard group centred on some of Wycliffe's colleagues at Oxford, the chief of whom was Nicholas of Hereford. In 1382 the Archbishop of Canterbury, William Courtney forced some of the Oxford Lollards to renounce their views and conform to Roman Catholic doctrine. Despite this setback, the sect continued to multiply among townsmen, merchants, gentry and even some of the lower clergy. Several knights of the royal household gave their support as well as a few members of the House of Commons. The strength of the Lollards during the last part of the 14th century was such that it was said that of every two men met on the roads one was sure to be a Lollard.

Many English kings would have welcomed the opportunity to dispossess the Church, using the rooting out of the undoubted corruption as an excuse to enrich themselves. It was the fear of throwing the realm into chaos that held them back. John of Gaunt who acted as head of government for much of this period, formed an odd alliance with Wycliffe probably as a counterbalance to the opposition of the clerics led by William Courtney. John of Gaunt died in 1399 and when Henry IV acceded to the throne in the same year, he needed the support of the Church and a wave of repression began against heresy. In 1401 the first English Statute was passed for the burning of heretics. The Lollard's first martyr William Sawtre of St Osythe was actually burned a few days before the Act was passed. Sir John Oldcastle, a leader of the Lollards and a supporter of Wycliffe, was arrested for heresy in 1413 and placed in the Tower of

London. He escaped but was captured four years later after conspiring with others to capture Henry V at Eltham Palace, Kent and take control of London. He was hanged and later burned in chains, the price for the double crimes of treason and heresy.

This repression brought an end to the Lollards' overt political influence. In an age when few could read, and the printing press had not come into use, if the Lollard preachers were killed or imprisoned their ideas were suppressed. Driven underground the movement operated henceforth chiefly among tradesmen and artisans, supported by a few clerical adherents. About 1500 a Lollard revival began and before 1530 the old Lollard and the new Protestant forces had begun to merge. The Lollard tradition facilitated the spread of Protestantism and predisposed opinion in favour of the Reformation, which was based on ideas deeply rooted in the English past.

The story of Ludchurch and the Lollards is that some of the Lollen men carried Wycliffe's Bible into the recesses of the Peak where they found eager listeners among the population. The area was thinly populated and some would live at such a distance from their Parish Church that they would rarely visit it. One day in the early 15th century, a congregation gathered in Ludchurch to hear Sir Walter De Ludauk preach. The King's men were in the locality, presumably because they had been forewarned that the Lollards were holding a service, and on hearing the singing they surrounded Ludchurch and called upon the congregation to yield in the king's name. Knowing their lives were in danger the Lollards drew their bows ready to give a good account of themselves. In the struggle that followed, Sir Walter's daughter Alice was killed by a crossbow bolt which had been aimed at the head forester Henrich Montair. Afterwards Alice's body was buried under an oak near the entrance to Ludchurch. Henrich Montair fled overseas to France but later joined Henry V at the battle of Agincourt. Sir Walter de Ludauk's fate is unknown but he may well have suffered that of the heretic.

Without the confirmation of the written record we will never know the reality of this sombre tale, but it has the ring of truth about it. Persecution may in the short term seem to suppress an idea but in the end it only strengthens it. To quote Victor Hugo; *'A stand can be made against invasion by an army: no stand can be made against invasion by an idea.'* By burning Wycliffe's books and imprisoning or executing the Lollard leaders, the power of the Lollards might seem to have been broken, but their ideas lived on in the minds of the people and eventually led to the establishment of the Church of England. King Henry VIII claimed to be a Catholic until his death, but Lollard ideas meant there was widespread support for his anticlerical legislation during the English Reformation.

In the Staffordshire Victoria Histories of the Counties of England is the following paragraph: *About 1862 the landowner, Philip Brocklehurst of Swythamley placed a ship's figurehead in the form of a woman at the entrance of Ludchurch. It was intended to commemorate the supposed martyrdom of the daughter of a Lollard preacher and was still there in 1914.*

William Bagshawe: Apostle of the Peak

Enough of highwaymen, rioters, murderers and scoundrels of that ilk. It is time to consider a man of the highest character who brought nothing but credit to his profession and the district. William Bagshawe was an outstanding Dissenting preacher whose whole vocation was spent in the Peak. He was born at Litton on the 17th January 1628 and baptised at Tideswell on the 29th of the same month. Thus he would have been a teenager during the English Civil War. After attending local country schools his education was completed at Corpus Christi College, Cambridge, where he took his B.A. degree in 1646.

Despite the strenuous opposition of his family, he was able to carry out the long cherished desire of becoming a Presbyterian minister, and on January 1st 1651 he was ordained at Chesterfield by the laying on of the hands of the presbyter. Immanuel Bourne, Rector of Ashover, acted as moderator. On leaving Oxford he entered the Ministry and was first Curate at Wormhill, near Buxton, where he preached his first sermon, and later at Attercliffe.

The opposition of his land-owning family is understandable considering the attitude of the landed classes to the clergy. Macaulay in describing the life of a clergyman of the period, wrote, *"During the century that followed the accession of Elizabeth, scarce a single person of noble descent took orders. A young levite might be had for his board, a small garret, and ten pounds a year, and might not only perform his own professional functions, might not only be the most patient of butts and listeners, might not only be always ready, in fine weather for bowls, and in rainy weather for shovelboards, but might also save the expense of a gardener and groom. Sometimes the reverend man nailed up the apricots; sometimes he curried the coach-horses. He cast up the farrier's bills. He walked ten miles with a message or parcel."* It is against this background that Bagshawe had determined to join the church. So strongly did his father object that he partially disinherited his son for his persistence. He received about one third as much of the family property as his younger brother John.

The year following his ordination, at the age of 23, he was inducted into the living at Glossop. On the 16th June 1650 he married Agnes Barker, daughter of Peter Barker of Darley. Two of their children, John and Samuel, were baptised at Glossop, whilst a third unnamed child was buried near the vestry door. William spent eleven happy years in the Parish of Glossop where he became exceedingly popular, concerning himself with the intellectual welfare of the people as well as their spiritual needs.

Glossop was fortunate in escaping the worst effects of the Civil War having nothing worthy of the name of a road passing through, or any castles or fortified manor houses meriting defence or attack, although some Glossop men did enlist on the Parliamentary side. The woollen cloth produced in the district would be carried westwards by packhorse to Manchester and Stockport which were Parliamentary strongholds and Glossop was largely of the same persuasion.

Whatever the views of William Bagshawe had been during the Civil War, the Restoration of Charles II in 1660 was to affect his way of life drastically. William was a leading member of the 'Presbyterian' establishment in Derbyshire and this was to set him at odds with the government of the day. After the re-establishment of the Monarchy, Parliament, with the intention of preventing further religious differences which it considered to have been one of the root causes of the Great Rebellion, passed the Act of Uniformity. This Act restricted the ministry of the Church to those who had received episcopal orders; the Book of Common Prayer was given legal status and the clergy were bound to use it.

This Act, amongst other requirements, called for every clergyman *"to read before this day, publicly, the morning and evening prayer from the revised Prayer Book, and to declare their unfeigned assent to everything contained in the book."* This was too much for many of the clergy; over 2,000 of them were of the opinion that to submit to the requirements of the Act would be to enslave their consciences. When they refused to take the prescribed oath they were expelled from their benefices. William Bagshawe was one of them, ejected from the living at Glossop on 'Black Bartholomew's Day', the 24th August 1662. His congregation wept at his last sermon, a testimony to the affection they had for him. The living remained vacant for some time and he was asked by his old parishioners to return but he dare not accede to their request.

Ford Hall, near Chapel-en-le-Frith.

Thirty nine livings were vacated at this time in Derbyshire; the following incumbents being within the High Peak: Thomas Shelmerdine, Matlock; Thomas Stanley, Eyam; Robert Cook, Monyash; John Beeley, Tideswell; William Naden, Fairfield; Edward Hollingshed, Ashford Chapel; and John Jackson; Buxton.

On being *'Cast out of my Parish at Glossop,'* as he put it, he went to live at his father's house, Ford Hall, near Chapel-en-le-Frith. The Bagshawes had been landowners in the Peak for hundreds of years. They were seated at Ridge Hall as early as AD 1141, and there 12 generations of the family spent their lives. An early Bagshawe was one of the King's foresters, as shown by the bugle horn that figures in their crest. John Bagshawe, William's younger brother, was High Sheriff of the County in 1696, in which position his influence no doubt helped William to escape the worst of the persecution. For some time after moving to Ford Hall he was obliged to act circumspectly. He attended the parish church at Chapel-en-le-Frith every Sunday morning and afternoon with his family. At night he preached privately in his own house and elsewhere. When some freedom of conscience was granted to the Non-conformists in 1672, he began to speak more publicly. To his Glossop congregation he managed to give a monthly lecture on weekdays. His successor at Glossop, Mr Sandiforth, was frequently one of his hearers, which says much for the power and conviction of his preaching.

His estate was sufficient to allow him the life of a country gentleman, but he preferred to continue preaching. Much of this was done privately, but the political oppression waxed and waned and during favourable times he was able to speak in public. The Conventicle Act of 1664 and the Five-Mile Act a year later resulted in non-conformists meeting behind locked doors or in isolated places on the moors where informers could not approach them without being spotted by the look-outs. Several warrants were issued for the arrest of William Bagshawe, but on every occasion he escaped, or the warrants were quashed by the magistrates who would know him well, coming from the same social background. In Charlesworth, not far from Long Lane, is a hollow known as the Glory Hole which was a secret place of worship of the Dissenters. Another was the remote Alport Farm in Hope Woodlands (SK 135911).

In 1672 when war against the Dutch seemed imminent, Charles II thought it best to conciliate all sections of the community. This was achieved by the Declaration of Indulgence, by which all forms of dissenting worship were allowed. Under the terms of this declaration licences were needed for preachers and also for meeting places. As a result, applications for these poured in from all around the country. William Bagshawe was granted a licence as a Presbyterian preacher on the 18th April 1672 and several places in the Peak were licensed as meeting places; he was the recognised preacher at all of them. William erected a chapel in the hamlet of Malcoff close to Ford Hall and he preached there regularly and also to the presbyterian communities in Chinley, Great Hucklow, and other villages in the Peak.

During the years he had been Vicar at Glossop he had made many friends and converts in the parish, and these supported him secretively, for it was against the law to meet openly for worship. During the last 26 years of his life he had the satisfaction of seeing the cause he had so much at heart firmly established at Chinley, from whence it spread to surrounding villages. In less than 12 months the Declaration was withdrawn and non-conformists were driven underground again. It is however from 1672 that non-conformist congregations date, since when they have had a continuous existence.

The next monarch, James II, twice issued and twice withdrew similar declarations and thus the position of William Bagshawe and non-conformists changed in a bewildering fashion. It is quite remarkable how those in authority never learn. The early Christian Church continued to grow despite the most ferocious persecution. During these two reigns several attempts were made to ascertain the number of non-conformists in the country. In 1669 town constables were required to furnish the information. The report of William Newsome, constable of Glossop, makes interesting reading:"October 8th 1669. I have no popish recusants, nor grayhounds, nor quakers, nor guns to the best of my knowledge within my liberty." In 1676 a census revealed 52 non-conformists at Glossop, but in 1682 only one, a Robert Bagshawe, admitted to that 'crime'.

After the Toleration Act of William and Mary of 24th May 1689, the time of William Bagshawe was fully taken up with preaching in nearly every town, village and hamlet in the Peak, travelling on horseback. Not until forced by advanced age did he curtail his journeys, and then many of his scattered congregation travelled to his home to hear him. The more liberal attitude following the Toleration Act is well illustrated by the fact that it was not until 1709 that the Charlesworth Independent Chapel bothered to apply for a licence.

During his latter years he produced 50 volumes including a work called *'De Spiritualibus Pecci, or notices concerning the work of God, and some of those who have been workers together with God,* in the Hundred of the High Peak'. A Justice of the Peace who was a thoroughly conforming member of the Church of England, said of him, *"I do not think St Paul himself was a better man than Mr Bagshawe, abating the inspiration, which was not to be reckoned amongst his personal virtues."*

During the whole of this period, both in the times of adversity under Charles II, during the brief indulgence of James II, and throughout the toleration of William III, William Bagshawe was most zealous as a preacher. The Presbyterian congregations at Malcoff, Hucklow, Bradwell, Charlesworth, Ashford, Middleton, Chelmorton and Bank End, were all founded and nurtured by his energy, discretion and devotion. He preached his last sermon at Ford Hall, March 22nd 1701, on the occasion of the death of his *"dear sovereign William of blessed memory,"* and he died on the 1st of the ensuing April.

At the time of writing, the Derbyshire Family History Society are making a record of the memorial inscriptions at the Charlesworth Top Chapel. Even the most cursory examination of the gravestones there reveals a surprising number of people from Glossop, Whitfield and further afield. I wonder how much this attachment stems from the ministry of William Bagshawe?

His will bearing the date October 15th 1701 contains the following provisions:

"As for my worldly goods I dispose thereof as follows:- Seeing that justice is every one's due I desire that my debts and heriots be paid; item, seeing that our charity should in some sort outlive us, I charge as a rent charge on those closes, enclosures and fields, lying within the precincts of Wormhill, now in the tenure of the children of Thomas Alsopp or Edward Torr as their guardian, the sum of fifty shillings yearly or year after year for ever to be paid out in pious and charitable purposes; to wit five shillings yearly for the poor of Litton where I first breathed, five shillings for the poor at or near Glossop and Chalsworth where I most exercised my most public ministry."

His ability as a preacher was described by John Ashe, his biographer as follows:

"He had a singular faculty for saying much in little. His words were close and piercing, and very often in the form of interrogations, which he thought more likely to move men than bare propositions. He spoke as one who felt what he said, and had a powerful sense upon his own mind of those things which he urged upon others. He also showed a peculiar dexterity in adapting his discourses to the dispensation of divine providence. He was mighty in the scriptures, his solutions of difficult passages were clear and satisfactory; his observations solid and judicious, and sometimes surprising and uncommon. Like a true son of Jacob, he wrestled with God and prevailed."

Some Peakland Churches

In addition to their primary purpose as centres of worship, our parish churches are important repositories of our history and as such well worth a visit, even if we only walk around God's Acre and read the inscriptions. After you have examined the epitaphs in local churchyards for some time, you are bound to be struck by the fact that some surnames are distinctly regional; Cooper, Booth, Thorpe, Eyre, Dewsnap, Hadfield, Bowden and Hall are just a few of the surnames you will find within the Peak; but take a trip say to Penistone and see how many are to be found there. You will find a very different selection. Presumably this is an indication of how few people moved far from their homes until relatively recently and it helps to explain the difference in local accents. Some of these surnames still seem to be concentrated in certain areas; take Ludlam for instance, very common in the south of the county yet virtually unknown in the Peak. If you were born in the Peak, you will be familiar with the expression used to scold anyone idling, "You are worse than Ludlam's dog!' This famous dog was reputed to be so idle that it lay down to bark. I have seen dogs do this very thing in Eyam and

Bakewell, so perhaps Derbyshire dogs have inherited this trait in their genes.

Fortunately many local churches have small booklets outlining something of the history of the church, objects of interest within and in the churchyard, and notable former residents. These are well worth purchasing for the information within and they also help to keep these buildings in existence so I hope you make a contribution in each church you visit. It is quite remarkable that in the Middle Ages, when most folks were struggling on the edge of poverty, they could manage to build such solid edifices which would stand for centuries, but today, for all our wealth, we seem unable to manage their upkeep. Some churches seem far too large for the present community and give some idea of the former importance of villages. Tideswell and Wirksworth were considerable centres in medieval times when Glossop and Buxton were mere backward hamlets. In the past, people left the land to seek better wages in the growing industrial towns, or were forced off by enclosures; and more recently the mechanisation of farming has meant that far less labourers are required. As one old farmer said to me,*"This valley used to support eight families when I was a boy, now we farm all of it."*

The medieval county of Derbyshire had only 109 churches, which, allowing for the difference in the size of the counties, was only half as many as Lincolnshire. In a thinly populated area such as the Peak some of the parishes were huge so that it was impossible for people to travel on foot to their parish church. This is sometimes revealed in the register of births, when five or six children in the same family were christened on the same day. It is easy to imagine the Vicar trying to persuade some farmer living perhaps twelve miles from the church, to bring his children in for baptism, and finally succeeding when a cart load could be assembled.

In 'The Compleat Angler' the following snatch of conversation describes the situation perfectly:

Viator: What have we here, a Church? As I'm an honest man, a very pretty
        church! Have you Churches in this country , sir?

Piscator: You see we have: but had you seen none, why should you make that
        doubt, sir?

Viator: Why, if you will not be angry, I'll tell you: I thought myself a stage or two
        beyond Christendom.

At the close of the 18th Century, pluralism was rampant in the Church, and it was not uncommon for a clergyman to hold several benefices, the parishes sometimes being situated in different counties. He might serve one of them in person, but in the others, he would place curates to whom small stipends would be given, and the rest of the emoluments would go in his own pocket.

John Wesley's Journal records several visits into the High Peak. Sometimes he was welcomed by the Vicar and allowed to preach in the Church as when he visited Hayfield in 1755 and 1757. On other occasions he spoke in the open air to crowds who flocked to hear him. In New Mills, a miller deliberately open the sluice of his water

Viators Bridge at Milldale, Alstonfield.

Wesley visiting nearby Staffordshire

wheel in an effort to drown Wesley's voice but all to no avail. His journal tells of several times when ruffians threw stones at him and missed, the missiles striking down his opponents in the crowd. Wesley saw it as proof of Divine favour that no brick hit him personally. Instead of addressing such matters as problems with tithes and vicars who rarely visited their parishes, the Established Church preferred at first to attack Wesleyan preachers. Rather than cast out the mote in their own eye, squires and parsons incited mobs to pelt John Wesley and in his diaries he noted how the gentry often headed the mob in person.

In William Chadwick's 'Reminiscences of Mottram' we learn that the Wesleyans were severely persecuted for a number of years. Parties collected together in groups to pelt the Dissenters on going to and leaving their places of worship, with mud, soil, stone and offensive eggs; and preachers who preached at the Cross were subjected to similar or even worse treatment. The huntsman was ordered to blow his horn in order to collect the hounds or hunting dogs to howl so as to prevent the preacher being heard by those who were desirous to listen to these Puritan ministers in the open air, entreating the people to turn away from their ways of wickedness and become followers of lowly Jesus. Men of the rudest habits were selected by the Vicar and other leading men of his party, to howl, shout, and drive these holy men out of the village.

In the 18th century substantial areas of Derbyshire lacked not only Anglican Churches, but Churches and Chapels of any kind. At the close of the century the parish of Hope had only two Churches for the hamlets of Bradwell, Brough, Shatton, Aston, Thornhill, Woodlands, Highlow, Offerton, Abney, Grange, Fernalegh, Wardlow, Stokehall, Grindlow, Great and Little Hucklow, Whaley, Doveholes and Fairfield; in all the parish extended over 40,000 acres. In 1832, the incumbent wrote to the Ecclesiastical Revenues Commissioners:

'I beg to state that there are no less than 18 hamlets in my parish, to make the tour of which I must travel six and thirty miles at least. Were it not for their vicinity to other Churches, or for Methodist Chapels, several of them would be without opportunities of attending Divine Worship in my Parish.'

In the same year the Vicar of Ashbourne pointed out that his parish was:

.....more than twenty miles in circumference; and that some of its hamlets are so distant from the only parish Church as not to be able to derive any benefit from attendance upon it. For instance the nearest point of the Hamlet of Hulland is upwards of four miles from Ashbourne.

In certain parts of the Peak manufacturing villages were springing up as mining, woollen and cotton spinning, lime burning and quarrying industries grew at a great rate, attracting migrants from various parts of the country and Ireland. In a belated effort to rectify a position where a large proportion of the labouring classes never went near a Church, many were built and dedicated; for example, Bradwell 1868; Buxton St John's 1840; Charlesworth 1849; Derwent 1867; and New Mills St George 1831.

There follows a brief selection of churches, all well worth a visit. Why not attend a service at one of them as part of your day in the Peak?

By looking at the columns in the nave of an English church it is possible to make a fair estimate of its age. If they are fat and round then the church is Norman or even Saxon dating from 1000 to 1200; if the columns are clustered then it indicates the decorated gothic period from 1200 to 1360. If the columns are of a geometrical cross section, perhaps octagonal then they are from the perpendicular gothic period from 1360 to 1450. Keep your eyes open for little details such as curiously carved gargoyles and the cressets which were the metal holders for the oil used in early lighting. Often only the cresset stones remain. The old fonts were usually deeper because it was the custom to fully immerse the child and in 1236 it was ordered that locked covers be provided for fonts to stop the theft of holy water.

St Peter's, Alstonefield

On entering the neat churchyard there is a phalanx of Beresford graves, but rather more unusual is the gravestone of Anne Green who died in April 1518, which must be one of the oldest dated headstones in the land. The practice of erecting memorial headstones only became common from the beginning of the 17th century and many of the early ones only have the initials of the deceased cut into them. The churchyard is graced with a fine and venerable yew tree which forms part of an arch as you approach the entrance. One of the limbs has been utilised to support an electric light. The entrance involves a rather awkward turn through a sort of vestibule which is doubtless intended to keep out the winter draughts.

Perhaps the most noteworthy feature once inside is the quality of the carving on the pews and the pulpit. For once, the man who did the work has left his name for posterity; on the back of the pews in the centre of the church is carved the legend, 'Edward Unsworth The Workeman'. The fine double decked pulpit is covered with similar carvings and a selection of religious texts.

To the left of the pulpit stands the Cotton family pew painted in a rather peculiar shade of green, complete with coat of arms coloured and gilt, why anyone should want to hide good oak panelling under paint is beyond me. It was made for Charles Cotton senior who owned Beresford Hall; his son Charles was a friend of Izaak Walton, author of The Compleat Angler. Its interior resembles a small railway compartment with the family members sitting facing each other.

At the rear of the church on the same side near the door, we find the opposite extreme; the pew for poor folks which consists of a few planks and these are rotten with woodworm. In the Middle Ages building a Church might take years and as styles of building changed so did the particular part under construction. Thus on the south side of Alstonefield church the pillars are of the Decorated period whilst those on the north are cruder in design and workmanship being built earlier. If you stand at the back of the church and look towards the altar it becomes obvious that the columns supporting the building are all leaning to the right. No doubt they have been like this for a few hundred years and are unlikely to fail before you reach the exit.

Ashbourne

Probably most impressive when approached along the A515 from Lichfield when the 14th century spire soaring to 212 feet can be seen to the finest advantage. The present Church was dedicated to Saint Oswald, King and Martyr in 1241, but there were Saxon and Norman churches on the site previously. Domesday Book records a priest and Church at Ashbourne in 1086. In these remote times the church would be the only public building and was used for meetings, and even dancing. There would be no pews for the common people, leaving the floor space open.

The Boothby Chapel contains tombs of the Cokayne family who held estates in Ashbourne from 1170, including Edmund slain at Shrewsbury in 1403 and another, Thomas 'The Magnificent', so nicknamed by Henry VIII for his appearance at the Field of the Cloth of Gold in 1520. Many visitors are drawn to Ashbourne church to see the recumbent white marble figure of Penelope Boothby who died in 1791 at the tender age of 5 years. The sculptor was Thomas Banks.

St Oswalds parish registers contain several entries of interest. Everyone knows about the visitation of the plague to Eyam, but what is less well known is that the plague struck many towns and villages in England over several centuries. Entries from 1586 to 1606 have the 'peste' or 'P' marked at the side; sometimes a whole family was struck down. Foundlings were named in an interesting manner; hence we have 1695, 16th September, Thomas Ashbourne, who was found at the alms houses a month before his baptism, or 1721, 20th March, Ashbourne Banks (a male child found there on the 19th).

All Saints, Bakewell

There were two priests to serve the Church at Bakewell when the value of the town was listed in the Domesday Survey which gives some indication of its importance since nowhere else in the Peak warranted such provision. The Church has Saxon and Norman origins and the large number of fragments remaining, some built into the existing edifice suggests a large early Church. Outside the south porch stand a row of stone coffins and within the porch the stone covers line one wall and stone fragments the other. The occupants of these stone coffins must have been of some importance when one considers the work involved in carving a coffin and lid from blocks of stone when most burials were enclosed only in a shroud.

The shaft of a fine Anglo-Saxon cross stands close to the Church and is believed to have once stood at a crossroads north of the town. Fine views of the spire can be obtained from various approaches and at closer range the fearsome looking gargoyles can be clearly made out. Inside is an early 19th century table of Church fees; for example a licensed marriage cost 10 shilling for the clergyman and 5 shillings for the clerk; a common headstone in the Churchyard cost 7 shillings; a tomb £3 3 shillings;

Alstonefield Church -"a stage or two beyond Christendom".

Cotton family pew, Alstonefield Church.

Poor folks pew, Alstonefield Church.

Alms Houses, Ashbourne.

there was no fee for christening. After exploring Bakewell Church make it your business before leaving the town to visit the Old House Museum which is a credit to the Bakewell Historical Society.

Chapel-en-le-Frith

In 1225 the Earl of Derby gave permission for the foresters to build a chapel in the forest at Chapel-en-le-Frith. The Chapel was built on the site of the present Church and was dedicated to Saint Thomas Becket. Traditionally the Church was consecrated on July 7th 1225 which as might be expected is the date associated with the local feasts and wakes. Saint Thomas was murdered on December 29th 1170, but was moved to a new shrine in Canterbury Cathedral on the 7th of July. Many Churches have lists of Vicars going back into the Middle Ages, but at St Thomas Becket a Mr Bramwell was appointed sexton in 1631 and the office was held by members of the same family until 1953. Just beyond the east end of the Church is a 13th century foresters grave; the stone has a crude carving of an axe, and over it the letters PL which appear to have been cut at a later date.

In 1648 the Church was used as a prison by Cromwell's troops to hold some 1,500 Scottish soldiers who had been captured at the Battle of Ribbleton Mill. During the fortnight they were incarcerated, 44 men died and were buried in the churchyard. The prisoners were then marched to Chester with more dying on the way. There are people in the Peak who claim to be of Scottish ancestry. They could well be the descendants of soldiers who decided not to go back after some raid into England, or of drovers who had passed through and made up their minds to tenant a small farm and stay.

The freeholders of Chapel-en-le-Frith have always clung tenaciously to their privilege of electing their own Vicar. Early in the 17th century a certain Thomas Barney attempted to install himself in the vicarage; as his predecessor was named Francis Barney it could be a case of a son trying to succeed his father. Depositions were taken at Chapel and numbers of elderly inhabitants told the same story that the right of election lay with the freeholders, that the chosen nominee was then presented to the Dean and Chapter of Lichfield for confirmation, and that the cost of keeping the Church in proper repair fell not upon the parishioners but upon the diocesan authorities. All were agreed that the Church was in a ruinous condition, so bad that " it was fearful and terrible for any to be in it or passe through," and one of the deponents "was moved to have set up a prop in it but durst not, lest it should have fallen upon his or their heads whilst it should be in doinge." Yet rather than contribute a penny to the cost of restoration, they were all quite willing to let the place fall into utter ruin.

St Lawrence, Eyam

The village of Eyam is best remembered for the visit of the plague in 1665-66, but this tale has been told too often to warrant further comment.

The Saxon Cross must be one of the best preserved in the land. This cross did not

CROSS IN EYAM CHURCH
YARD, DERBYSHIRE
From Chantrey's Peak Scenery 1886

CROSS IN BAKEWELL
CHURCH YARD,
DERBYSHIRE
From Chantrey's Peak Scenery 1886

always stand in the churchyard but was a wayside cross where itinerant priests or monks would preach when in the area. Like other wayside crosses it may have been cast down as the result of an Act of Parliament of 1643 which ordered the removal and destruction of crosses in public places. As the Eyam Cross is in such an excellent state, it seems likely that local folks circumvented the wishes of parliament by concealing it with the intention of re-erecting it when government policy changed as it was likely to do at short notice during the English Civil War. It is unfortunate that the top portion of the shaft is missing.

Eyam Church is worth a visit during the summer months if only because of the lectures and guided tours which are offered. The plague and its consequences are explained together with a tour of the church and its points of interest. The churchyard has several curiosities; there are two stone coffin lids reputed to be those of crusaders standing against the south wall outside the priest's door and the upper half of one of them has been built into the church wall near the organ. Immediately above the priest's door is a sundial constructed by William Shaw a local stonemason and dated 1775; this is one of the advantages of churches being built on an east-west axis, the south wall is ready made for mounting a vertical sundial. It is usual for gravestones to face east, but there are several at Eyam which face west. Another feature is the monument to William Wood, the local historian and author which bears the inscription:-

> 'Men but like visions are,
> Time all doth claim,
> He lives who dies and
> Leaves a lasting name.'

William Wood has come in for some criticism for historical inaccuracies and the moral nature of his stories. William Wood lived in Victorian times when this style of writing was all the rage. At the time of writing his books were popular and we owe him a debt of gratitude for recording so much.

A more unusual headstone is that of the Derbyshire cricketer, Harry Bagshaw. It has a bat, ball and stumps carved on it and the umpire's raised finger of dismissal. In the same grave lie his wife Jeannie who kept the George and Dragon besides Woodhead Reservoir until its closure and their son Eddie Wingfield who died in 1952.

St Michael's, Hathersage

Hathersage churchyard is the reputed last resting place of Robin Hood's lieutenant, Little John. According to Pilkington, in 1784 a human thigh bone 28 inches long was uncovered (in different accounts the length varies between 28 and 32 inches). If such a relic had been found it is hardly likely that it would just have disappeared. Brian Robinson in 'The Seven Blunders Of The Peak' suggests that the stones at each end of the grave marked out a medieval measure of length; the village perch, no less. Whatever the truth of the matter it is doubtful if careful excavation at this time would settle it once and for all. In any case, Hathersage and its Church are well worth a visit even if Robin Hood and company never came within bowshot.

St Matthew, Hayfield

A Church was founded on the present site when Richard II gave the land in 1386. The existing building erected in 1818 is not one of striking beauty but nevertheless has its points of interest. In the north gallery is a tablet to Joseph Hague surmounted by a bust. Joseph Hague was born in the hamlet of Chunal and is reputed to have made a great fortune in cloth trading, although there are those who hold that he made a large portion of it from the slave trade. Whatever the truth of the matter, having made his fortune he lived at Park Hall, Little Hayfield, and built the Hague School in Whitfield and endowed it with funds which are still administered by trustees to this day.

When John Wesley visited Hayfield, the incumbent was called John Baddeley. This Vicar was so popular with the free holders who elect their own Vicar, that they built him a parsonage and made out the deed of gift to Baddeley himself instead of to the Vicar of Hayfield. When the Vicar died, his daughters sold it and eventually it became the Royal Hotel.

John Wesley's visit to Hayfield on July 23rd, 1748, coincided with a terrible flood, not the first or last to strike Hayfield. In his journal he wrote:

"There fell for about three hours, a very heavy rain, which caused such a flood as had not been seen by any now living in those parts. The rocks were loosened from the mountains; one field was covered with huge stones from side to side. Several water mills were clean swept away, without leaving any remains. The trees were torn up by the roots and whirled away like stubble.

Two women of loose character were swept away from their own door and drowned. One of them was found near the place; the other was carried seven or eight miles. Hayfield Churchyard was all torn up, and the dead bodies swept out of their graves to be deposited at the doors of the living. When the flood abated, they were found in several places. Some were hanging in trees; others left in meadows or grounds; some partly eaten by dogs, or wanting one or more of their members."

Anyone who fell asleep during a long boring sermon at Hayfield was liable to need the attention of the 'Sluggard Waker'. This important official carried a long staff with a knob at one end to rap the men and a feather at the other to tickle the women.

The most remarkable event claimed to have been witnessed at Hayfield appears in a letter dated 1745:

"The indecent custom still prevails of burying the dead in a place set aside for devotions. On the last day in August several hundreds of bodies rose out of the grave in the open day to the astonishment and terror of several spectators. They deserted the coffins and arising out of the grave ascended vertically towards

Stone coffins on display, Bakewell Church and below,
a collection of stone coffin lids inside the entrance to the church.

heaven singing. They had no winding sheets yet did not appear naked. Their vesture seemed streaked with gold and interlaced with sable and they left behind a fragrant and delicious odour and were quickly out of sight. What became of them or where their residence may be, no mortal can tell".

The bridge over the River Sett close by Hayfield Church is of unusual construction in that the foundations at one end are built upon bales of wool, a distinction that it shares with the Old London Bridge.

St Peter's, Hope

Hope was another of the few places in the Peak which had a priest and a Church at the time of the Domesday Survey. Nothing remains of the Saxon Church which might well have been built from wood. One of the most striking things about Hope Church is the skill of the men who laid the stone paving slabs in the nave - almost level enough to play billiards on. Other interesting relics from the past are two 13th century forester's tombstones which were discovered when the chancel was rebuilt in the 19th century. They are believed to be those of the Woodroffe family, or Wood-reeves with early English crosses and forester's axes. Their tapered shape suggests that they were once the lids of stone coffins like the ones outside Bakewell Church. The Saxon cross near the south aisle dates from the time of King Alfred, and was hidden in the fabric of Hope School from the English Civil War until 1850. Thomas Bocking was Vicar and Schoolmaster at that time and his schoolmaster's chair bears the date 1664 and a Latin motto which translates as "You cannot make a scholar out of a block of wood."

In early 1530 two Bradwell men created an unseemly scene inside the parish church at Hope engaging in fisticuffs before the altar. Why they couldn't have settled matters outside is unknown but Robert Elott maliciously struck Edmund Elott on the nose before the altar of Saint Nicholas and blood was effused upon the altar. No time was lost in certifying such a terrible event to the Chapter, the three who took the oath as having witnessed the outrage being Otwell Bamford, Curate of Hope, Nicholas Smyth, and Helia Staley. Robert Elott confessed, whereupon the Chapter appointed Canon Edmund Stretehay to act as their commissary, and Robert was brought to his knees in more ways than one, for the Canon ordered him to submit to corporal punishment, kneeling before him.

When blood was shed in the church there was a great to do; the sacred edifice having been defiled, service was not allowed until that defilement had been wiped out; and in this case the church was closed for two months. The Bishop's Chancellor was informed of the circumstance, and he inhibited the Curate from celebrating in the church until episcopal reconciliation had been obtained.

St Bartholomew's, Longnor

Any old churchyard is worth a visit and the one at Longnor is no exception. The gravestones in the churchyard are notable for the fineness of the carving. I am not sure

Woodcutter's Grave, Chapel-en-le-Frith Churchyard

Chapel Market Cross

Crusader's Coffin lids Eyam - possibly members of the Stafford family.

Eyam Sundial.

whether this is due to the skill of the masons or the quality of the local stone. Every inscription has a story to tell, even if it is only the dreadful child mortality of the past. The churchyard has several stones which face west instead of east and the grave inscriptions alone are worth a closer study. I particularly like the one on the grave of William Billinge which reads as follows;

In Memory of William Billinge, who was born in a Cornfield at Fawfieldhead in this Parish in the year 1679. At the age of 23 years he enlisted into His Majesty's Service under Sir George Rooke, and was at the taking of the Fortress of Gibraltar, in 1704. He afterwards served under the Duke of Marlborough at the ever Memorable Battle of Ramillies, fought on the 23rd, of May, 1706. where he was wounded by a musket shot in the thigh. He afterwards returned to his native country and with manly courage defended his Sovereign's rights at the Rebellion in 1715 and 1745. He died within the space of 150 yards of where he was born, and was interred here the the 30th of January, 1791, aged 112 years.

Billited by Death, I quartered here remain.
When the trumpet sounds, I'll rise and march again.

(William would have been sixty six at the time of the 1745 rebellion.)

Or what of Samuel Fidler, of Longnor who died in 1780, aged 105 years? *"Walked from his home to Buxton within three days of his death, which is upwards of five miles."* And Jane Simms, aged 22 years? *"Who unintentionally effected an ignominious exit of her inglorious career on the 21st day of April, 1830."* What sad story lies behind this epitaph?

The booklet describing Saint Bartholomew's, Longnor contains a paragraph which illustrates the state of the Church of England during one of its lowest phases. Some Rectors, especially those with multiple benefices, were unpopular because of the tithe system, and of course there were those who could hardly be held up as an example of good living. Under such circumstances, it was scarcely surprising that folks flocked to hear John Wesley and his lieutenants as they travelled the country.

In the 18th Century, spiritual life in the area was at a low ebb, drunkenness flourished, as did illegitimacy. According to a vivid contemporary Methodist description of Longnor and its Church life, *"The state of morals being so profane, sensual and brutal in character that sin ceased to blush.....few attended public worship....and in their eagerness to lose as little time as possible by devotion, the men have been known to take the football into Church; and as soon as the Benediction was pronounced it was thrown down in the very Sanctuary; when the conductor of the worship would commence the unhallowed sport."*

Mellor

December 1810. A note in the register by the Vicar of Mellor which shows how important a force Methodism was at that time:

'The number of baptisms here is diminished of late through the Methodist Preachers taking it upon them to baptise and to administer the Lord's Supper tho' formerly they professed to be Members of the Church of England, and tho' Mr Wesley severely rebuked them for attempting to usurp the right of administering either of the sacraments, being mere laymen. Ever since my coming here most of the illegitimate children have been taken for baptism to some other of the Separatists in order that the lewd mothers might escape a serious Admonition.'

M. Olerenshaw.

Mottram

Tradition has it that the mortar used in the construction of Mottram Church was mixed with strong ale. There is another story which goes the rounds from time to time to the effect that a local benefactor left a strip of land six graves wide in Mottram churchyard so that any local man who died of hard work could have free burial, and that to date the strip remains empty. I have to tell you from personal experience that there is not a word of truth in this assertion. Having lived in Mottram for several years and realising that I was an ideal candidate, a trip was made up the hill to see Canon Reginald Sutcliffe Roch and get my name on the list. Alas, the story turned out to be a pure fabrication.

Another interesting tale concerns one Vicar of Mottram who was said to have had a wife with a nose like a pig's snout, and who ate from a silver trough. This was claimed to be a judgement on her mother who once saw a poor woman with a number of little children come to her door to beg and in her sinful pride and scorn exclaimed, "Just see yon old sow with her litter after her."

In the registers at Mottram Church there is a record of Hamnett Hyde, the curate, going to Greenwich to be touched by King James I on 27th of May 1610. It had been believed for centuries that the kings of England could cure scrofula, also known as the 'King's Evil', just by touching a sufferer, or by allowing them to use water in which he had bathed.

The inscription on the grave from which the body had been stolen by resurrection men at Mottram has been mentioned elsewhere, but here is an epitaph which gives a glimpse of life for the reasonably well to do who liked nothing better than to pursue a fox or hare across the countryside.

IN AFFECTIONATE REMEMBRANCE OF
GEORGE NEWTON OF STALEYBRIDGE
WHO DIED AUGUST 7th 1871 in his 94th year

Though he lived long the old man's done at last
No more he'll breathe the huntsman's stirring blast
Though fleet as Reynard in his youthful prime
At length he's yielded to the hand of time

William Wood Memorial

Saxon Cross, Hope

Hope Church entrance

Tideswell Church

Blithe as a lark dressed in his coat of green
With hounds and horn the gallant man was seen
But ah death came worn out and full of years
He died in peace mourned by his offsprings tears

Stoney Middleton

Driving down Middleton Dale along the main road with lorry loads of limestone roaring past, it would be easy to dismiss the village as a place best passed through quickly and forgotten. This would be a mistake, because if you can find somewhere to park your vehicle and take a walk towards the church you will be pleasantly surprised. Once off the main road, every cottage seems to be brightened with hanging baskets of flowers and the gardens are bright as is only to be expected on a limestone soil. The village Church of St Martin is unusual because it is built in an octagonal pattern, the only one in Derbyshire.

The Church at Stoney Middleton was without a Vicar for a considerable period during the nineteenth century until one day the Bishop of Lichfield and his entourage stopped in the village to dine at the Moon Inn. Once they had started their meal, the Landlord said to the Bishop, *"The Wesleyans hereabouts say that they are the only ones to preach God's word to the sinners of Stoney Middleton, since we have no Vicar."*

The Bishop was somewhat taken aback on receiving this intelligence, but after a few moments reflection replied, *"I will make it my business to appoint a Vicar to the living as soon as possible so that you can go to church once more."*

"Not on my account, I never go to Church." said the Landlord, unabashed.

Despite this unpromising reception, the Bishop kept his word and appointed the Rev Urban Smith in 1834.

St John The Baptist, Tideswell

A magnificent parish church built entirely in the 14th century; there have been no additions to the fabric since 1400, which means that its construction must have been seriously interrupted by the Black Death around 1349. Although not a vast building, Tideswell Church is often described as the Cathedral of the Peak. The fine interior is equally suggestive of a small cathedral with rich carving in the choirstalls and misericord seats. There is no shortage of monuments of historical interest; in the chancel is the tomb chest of Sir Sampson Meverell, a veteran of the Hundred Year's War who fought in twelve battles in France and there are brasses to Bishop Pursglove and to members of the Foljambe family. The chancel is the crowning glory of the Church, beautifully spacious and lit by the 'Jesse' east window which tells the story of John the Baptist. This window dates from 1875 and is another example of the excellent restoration work carried out by the Victorians. The age of the Church shows in the state of stonework around the main entrance and elsewhere; considerable sums will have to spent in preserving the building. Fortunately one great advantage of a stone building over say, a modern reinforced concrete one, is that skilled masons can replicate the original stones and replace them individually.

St Mary The Virgin, Wirksworth

The Church stands in its churchyard hidden from the main road by a row of houses. The interior contains a remarkable collection of Norman stone carvings which have been set into the walls in a random manner, almost as if you were expected to seek them out. They include a depiction of a king and queen, animals, even a pair of legs and a great favourite, the figure of a Derbyshire lead miner marching along with his pick over his shoulder. This last was apparently found at Bonsall and incorporated in the Church in 1876. The most intricate is The Wirksworth Stone which was found in 1820 when the pavement in front of the altar was being removed; the clarity of the carving has been preserved by its long sojourn in the soil. The size of the Church is some indication of the former importance of Wirksworth when it was a thriving centre of the lead mining industry.

Woodhead

St James' at Woodhead must be one of the most remote Chapels in England standing at around 800 feet above sea level high in the Longdendale Valley. In 1487 Sir Edmund Shaa, Lord Mayor of London, left a sum of money to pay for a priest in the Chapel he had made in Longdendale which suggests that the little chapel is a few years older. Being born locally, Sir Edmund would be aware of the difficulties facing travellers crossing the Pennines at this point before roads were built. In the circumstances it is remarkable that the chapel has survived at all as it has always been dependent on local farmers for its upkeep. The population can never have been large even before the building of the reservoirs led to the destruction of many farms.

The construction of the Woodhead Railway Tunnel in the middle of the 19th century meant a huge influx of navvies into the valley, but there would be few of them interested in visiting the local Chapel although several of them who died during the cholera outbreak are buried there. Others who died of cholera at the same time were buried further down the valley at Tintwistle Church and if you look in the North-east corner of the graveyard you will find an area covered with ling. Popular tradition has it that this is the spot where the cholera victims were buried and that is why it has not been used since. As the tunnel connected Cheshire with Yorkshire disputes arose as to which priest was responsible for administering the last rites to injured workmen. Understandable, when to visit a dying man meant being lowered 400 feet into the bowels of the earth in a bucket, relying on the driver of the steam engine at the surface and trying to find the way with a paraffin lamp. There must have been a strong temptation to wait until he was dead and his body brought to the surface.

Woodhead Chapel suffered yet another blow to its existence in late 1994 when wretches stole the stone slates from the roof.

The gravestone of William Billinge at Longnor.

The Wirksworth stone, which depicts a variety of religious scenes.

A Derbyshire Millstone -
All that remains of the Bone Mill in Chunal, which stood just below the Grouse Inn.

Carving of a Derbyshire lead miner from Wirksworth Church. Was he heading for the nearest riots?

Youlgreave

Not to be missed, certainly one of the finest Churches within the Peak. The nave is striking with its pillars and arches which are different on each side. The three bays separating the nave from the south aisle are typically late Norman with stout round pillars and round arches; The equivalent arcade on the north side shows a change of style. The pillars are lighter with finer carved floral designs and animal and human heads, while the arches are in the pointed Gothic style. Here is an example of building going on over a period of years and the work being carried out in the current style. Not only are the two sets of arcades different in style, but they are not positioned with the pillars opposite each other. Despite this lack of symmetry, the finished nave has a beauty of its own.

The great difference between medieval churches and the ones built in Victorian times are the fine collections of brasses, plaques, tombs of former Lords of the Manor which fill the older churches, while the Victorian churches are more likely to have a memorial to some wealthy mill owner who as like as not paid for most of its construction in the same manner as his land-owning predecessor. Youlgreave has some fine examples, for instance the Jacobean wall memorial to Roger Rooe of Alport showing the knight and his wife kneeling facing one another across a prayer desk with their eight children lined up below. Mrs Rooe looks a very stern lady with her tall hat and beautifully carved ruff.

To the right of this monument is a window dated some 300 years later to the memory of Rennie Crompton Waterhouse of Lomberdale Hall, Middleton-by-Youlgreave, who was killed at Gallipoli in 1915. It contains glass collected by his brother from the destroyed cathedral of Ypres. Here we have the very essence of history.

The parish registers contain several entries of interest:

'Our most gracious soveraigne Lady Elizabeth quene of England, France and Ireland departed this lyffe uppon Wednesday being 23rd of March 1602 after she had reigned most peaceablye 44 yeares, 4 moneths, 11 daies.'

Elizabeth's reign was hardly the most peaceable in English history, but in Youlgreave the turmoil could easily have passed virtually unnoticed. At a more mundane level we find:

For whipping the dogs forth of the church in tyme of divyne service. 1 shilling and 4 pence', and the record of a severe winter:

"This year 1614/15 January 16th, began the greatest snow which ever fell uppon the earth, within man's memorye. It covered the earth fyve quarters deep upon the playne. And for heaps or drifts of snow, they were very deep; so that passengers, both horses and foot, passed over gates, hedges and walles. It fell at 10 severall tymes and the last was the greatest, to the greate admiration and feare of all the land, for it came from the fowre pts of the world, so that all entryes

The Rooe Memorial, Youlgreave Church,
dedicated to Roger Rooe, his wife and their eight children.

Youlgreave Church - stout Norman pillars and round arches on the south side of the nave, built between 1150 and 1170, and below, on the north side of the aisle lighter pillars support Gothic arches built at a later date.

were full, yea, the south pte as well as these mountaynes. It continued by day encreasing untill the 12th day of March (without the sight of any earth, eyther uppon hilles or valleyes) uppon which day (being the Lord's Daye) it began to decreasse; and so by little and little consumed and wasted away, till the eight and twentyth day of May for then all the heapes or drifts of snow were consumed, except one uppon Kinder's Scout, which lay till Witson week and after. There fell also ten lesse snowes in Aprill, some a foote deep, some lesse, but none continued long. Uppon May day in the morning, instead of fetching flowers, the youthes brought in flakes of snow, which lay above a foot deep upon the moores and mountaynes."

Most parish registers are now lodged in the County Record Office at Matlock where they can be examined at leisure. They are a source of endless fascination beyond the immediate interest of the genealogist. Road accidents are nothing new; you will find records of people being run over by horse drawn wagons, or falling from wagons after falling asleep. Stage coaches were particularly dangerous with passengers falling off the top and being 'dashed to pieces.' A surprising number came to an unhappy end by falling from a bicycle when drunk. This may be a reflection on the state of the roads rather than the fondness of the victims for strong ale. There are plenty of records of vagrants dying of starvation and jaggers being frozen to death when trapped together with their teams of pack horses on the moor tops in a blizzard.

Stage Coach in MIDDLETON DALE From Chantrey's Peak Scenery 1886

30 ft Snowdrifts in the Peak: Chronicle 31.3.1916.

A severe blizzard raged over the Peak District on Tuesday. For 6 hours snow fell very heavily, especially in the Hope Valley, and the full force of the blizzard was felt at Bradwell, Bamford and Castleton. Snow lay to a great depth on the high lands.

The Sheffield and Manchester road over the Snake Moors to Glossop is still blocked, as it has been a month. During that time no vehicular traffic has passed between Glossop and the Woodlands where there are drifts 16 to 30 ft high. The highway authorities 3 weeks ago engaged men from Bradwell, Bamford and Castleton to cut a road, but the work had to be abandoned. Men cannot be got to open up the rest of the road and there are big avalanches overhanging the existing cuttings, threatening to fall upon those who travel along.

March 1986 - the Snake Pass was blocked for weeks by this cliff of ice, pieces of which kept breaking off and rolling down onto the road.

The Bradwell Fever

The great Plague which attacked Eyam in 1666 and killed between a quarter and a third of the population (this proportion is seriously questioned today), has caught the public imagination, in particular the idea that the inhabitants following the lead of their Vicar William Mompesson volunteered to stay in the village and thus prevent the disease spreading beyond its confines. However, it is much more likely that they were prevented from leaving by their neighbours once the nature of the disease was realised. The Duke of Devonshire would doubtless regard it as a sound investment to supply them with food in exchange for keeping to Eyam. There are plenty of examples from elsewhere in the country of such a quarantine being imposed. A typical example comes from the oral

A well kept corner of 'Bradda'.

An old Bradwell house sinking back into the earth from whence it came.

tradition of the Hepworth Plague. From "History of Kirkburton and Graveship of Holme" by Henry James Moorhouse: 1861, pages 197-8 *'A family called Beevers living in the south part of Hepworth received a package from London at the time of the Plague. The Beevers and several of their neighbours died shortly afterwards. People living in the north of Hepworth realising what was the matter, erected a fence to keep the infected people in.'*

The epidemic which broke out in Bradwell in 1869 was not so dreadful, but still must be regarded as a very serious affair. The fever broke out towards the end of 1869 and the first to suffer were those residing in the lower parts of the town, in Bridge Street, Nether Side, Church Street and Town Bottom.

Many and varied suggestions were put forward as to the cause of the contagion, but its origin is still a mystery, although some attributed it to bad drainage, because all the filthy water settled and stagnated in the sewers at the lower end of the village, in the immediate vicinity of the outbreak of the pestilence. This argument received support from the fact that no fresh cases were reported after a heavy flood had completely washed out the sewers and water courses.

At first some thought that the fever was typhus, some typhoid, and yet others gastric, and it is possible that the treatment of the patients for one kind of fever when really suffering from another might be the cause of so many deaths in the former part of the visitation. However, when the doctors found out the true nature of the epidemic and treated it accordingly, the death rate was much smaller. On the 31st of March, 1869, as the plague showed no signs of abatement, and many deaths were occurring daily, the town was fumigated with tar, and the sewer mouths with copperas (ferrous sulphate), while all the manure heaps were cleared away. Despite these efforts the following month saw a rise in the number of fatalities and notwithstanding all exertions the fever continued its ravages through the summer and autumn. On the 27th of October a deputation from the Bakewell Sanitary Authority - consisting of Lord Denman, Dr Fentem, Dr Taylor, and Inspector Williams inspected the town, and the nuisance inspector paid another visit on the 16th of November. Not surprisingly the inhabitants were panic stricken by the virulence of the scourge, and great hardship prevailed in many homes. To relieve the more needy, Mr J K Cocker of Hathersage, on the 22nd of December kindly sent fifty stones of flour, and this was distributed amongst the poorest of the villagers. One widow whose case was exceptionally distressing, had by special orders five stones, and the remaining forty-five were equally divided amongst thirty people.

The outbreak of fever is often attributed to lack of cleanliness, but it is unlikely that this was the cause in this instance, as the inhabitants of Bradwell were a thrifty, striving and cleanly people, while the houses of both high and low, rich and poor, were alike stricken by the terrible disease. The following numbers of victims come from the diary of a local man. Unfortunately they do not include figures for the end of 1868 or beginning of 1870:

1869:

January; 3 attacked and recovered	July; 24 attacked and 4 died
February; 6 attacked and 5 died	August; 5 attacked and recovered
March; 5 attacked and 4 died	September; 18 attacked and 4 died
April; 12 attacked and 5 died	October; 16 attacked and 6 died
May; 15 attacked and 1 died	November; 20 attacked and 3 died
June; 9 attacked and 6 died	December; 19 attacked and 3 died.

It will thus be seen that out of a population of some 1000, 152 were attacked in the year, 41 of that number succumbed to the disease. This pestilential outbreak is still spoken of and will be long remembered in local history as the Bradwell Fever.

Remarkable Pauperism 12.12.1874.

Some years ago there resided at Eyam a poor woman seventy years of age, and it was calculated that the amount of parochial relief received by her from the township, for her own personal and individual maintenance was £506 1s. 6d.

Tideswell 6.10.1877.

At 3 am on Saturday last the inhabitants of High Street were aroused with the cry "House on fire". Soon a band of workers were at the house of Mr Samuel Middleton, baker. The doors and windows were at once broken open and sufficient water thrown to get the fire under, before an attempt could be made to look for Mr Middleton. At length a search was made and he was found in the back chamber almost lifeless. The damage done by the fire would have been greater if the contents had not been of oak. The clock weights were molten into a cake of lead and the furniture was burnt to ashes and the ceiling plaster had fallen down.

A Few Tall Tales

In just about any village they can tell you a few stories to illustrate the stupidity of the neighbours, but Tideswell seems to have drawn a fine selection. Thus a Tideswell man might be greeted with, *"Who sawed the calf's head off when it got stuck in the gate?"*

Place names are not always pronounced exactly as they are written; Tintwistle is known locally as Tinsel, Tideswell on the other hand, is known to the natives as Tidser or Tidsa. A Tidser man is reputed to have put a pound of tallow candles in a hot oven to dry them. Other exploits accredited to the natives are lying under a wheelbarrow to paint the underside and then carrying it for three miles to deliver to the owner. Putting a nosebag on the horse before turning it out to graze and erecting wire netting to keep out the dreaded small-pox. One old dame lifted her pig to the top of the wall one Whit-Monday so that it could see the Friendly Societies annual procession.

Another Tidserite is reputed to have dug a well and when faced with the problem of where to get rid of the earth, promptly set to to dig another well to hold it.

"Which way is it to Tideswell?" asked a tourist who was within sight of the parish church.

"Dust see yon church? Well that's Tidser. Ask 'em to tell thee theer."

Some of the best stories could have come straight out of Chaucer's Canterbury Tales. A Tideswell carrier who had just moved to a new district was undecided as to the quality of the ales in the neighbourhood. At the first village pub he came to he flicked his whip at the window to gain the attention of the landlord. The pot-bellied landlord came scurrying out with a beaming smile.

"They tell me you have some decent ale here Mester," said the carrier.

"I reckon we have some of the best ale in the village," replied the landlord.

"Well, bring us a quart."

After draining the measure, the carrier sympathetically remarked, *"It's been no so bad, bring me another."* The second quart went the same way as the first and then the carrier pointedly observed, *"It's been no so bad; tha didna lie. I'll come in and have a sup."*

A Tideswell poultry farmer had three wooden huts, each of which contained about a hundred fowls. One morning on visiting the field he found that one of his sheds, complete with fowls had disappeared. The next morning when he went to feed the poultry he found that the second shed had gone as well. On returning to the house he told his wife who was extremely angry and said, *"If you don't do something about it we shall be bankrupt."*

So the farmer went to the field after nightfall and, taking his camp stool and his double-barrelled gun, he settled down in the hen house to await events. For a long time nothing happened, he heard the church clock strike the midnight hour but not another sound. Shortly afterwards the hen-house began to shake violently and rock from side to side until the farmer thought a terrible storm had arisen. Finally he could stand it no longer and grasping his gun firmly in both hands and with his finger on the trigger, he pushed the door open with his foot and on stepping out he fell ....off a lorry.

Tideswell was formerly famous for the manufacture of very hard cheeses. An old gentleman bought one of these cheeses but he couldn't cut it, or break it, or even make a hole in it either. As a last attempt he carried the armour plated cheese to the top of Tideswell church tower and threw it over the top hoping for the best. It so happened that an old and very poor couple lived opposite the church tower and at that very moment were praying for food, or at least the money to buy it, when the case-hardened cheese crashed down on a gravestone slab, bounced over the churchyard wall, trundled across the road and finally came to rest inside the living room of the old folks cottage. And so it came to pass that the poor people's prayer was answered and the old man turned to his wife and said, *"Ah wench; tha sees the good Lord's sent us a cheese."* We are never told how, or whether, they managed to eat it.

A couple of Tideswell hay-dealers, after delivering hay some distance away, were returning late at night and lost and their way. After calling at various wayside taverns to refresh their horse they came to a cross roads where there was a signpost, but it was too dark to see what was painted on the finger post, and the only one who could read was a small boy who was with them. His father told him to climb the post giving him some matches and told him to see what he could make of it after giving him a leg up. After striking a few lucifers the lad called out, *"I can't read it feyther, the letters are too big."*

Don't laugh too loudly at the simple souls in Tideswell. A Glossop man was asked by a neighbour when was he going to tar his shed. Shortly afterwards he started to boil the tar in a wooden bucket on the house fire and managed to burn the place to the ground. Not surprisingly he had great difficulty afterwards in finding a landlord prepared to let him rent a house.

Many years ago when the idea of parachutes became a reality, a young chap who lived at the top of the steep section of Queen Street in Glossop decided to make his own. This bright idea was achieved by chopping up his mother's clothes line, borrowing one of her sheets and attaching lengths of clothes line to each corner. When the contraption was ready, he launched himself from the bedroom window into a strong south-westerly. Instead of coming to rest gently in the street, he was swept away and ended up in in a heap in Wren Nest Mill yard.

Once upon a time there was a farmer in a Peakland township who allowed locals to picnic on his land by the brook and cheerfully let them light a bonfire there on Guy Fawke's night. Children played among the trees and in the brook on long summer's nights. God was in his heaven and everyone lived in harmony. Alas, one day the farmer died and his son took over the farm. What a change, the new tenant was a belligerent fellow who delighted in chasing folks off his property, thinking nothing of discharging a shotgun over their heads and delighting in putting a ferocious bull in the field.

One day, he was enraged to see a yellow tent at the bottom of one of his fields, so down he rushed like a charging rhinoceros, and without pausing for an instant to enquire into whose tent it was, or why it might be there, ripped it up and threw it together with its contents over a wall and into a deep quarry.

Feeling well satisfied with these exertions he returned to the farm. Alas, his self congratulations were premature, waiting there were a couple of officers from the Ordnance Survey who had come to let him know that they would be working across his land during the next few days and had pitched their tent together with some valuable instruments near the quarry. It was an expensive business replacing the damaged equipment. Such a misfortune could not have happened to a more deserving chap.

Customs, Antiquities, and Distractions

Shrove-Tuesday Football

The only similarity between Association Football and the Shrove-Tuesday game is that a ball features in both. There are those who claim that the game was introduced by the Romans, presumably to provide some light relief from throwing Christians to the lions. One thing is certain, the game is of great antiquity. (Mary Queen of Scots watched a football game between members of her retinue and the garrison from the ramparts of the castle at Carlisle). A stranger coming across this frightful struggle could be excused for thinking he had stumbled upon some ferocious form of tribal warfare. Glover describes the game in the following terms, *"broken shins, broken heads, torn coats, and lost hats are among the minor accidents in this fearful contest."* At one time the old game was popular in many parts of the country, but today only lingers in a few spots such as Atherstone, Workington and best of all at Ashbourne. Injuries are rightly regarded as self-inflicted and thus debar those receiving them from drawing benefits from the Friendly Society.

At Ashbourne the combatants consist of the Uppards and the Downards whose objective is to convey a ball stuffed hard with wood shavings through the opposing goal. The Uppards goal is at Sturton Mill while the Downards is two and a half miles away at Clifton Mill. Prior to 1860 the ball was tossed up in the Market Place and the battle began. In that year the authorities decided to suppress the ancient game, and several players were summoned by the police under a section of the Highways Act, and they were convicted by the magistrates. The players took their case to the Court of the Queen's Bench but lost once more. Despite the Decision of the Queen's Bench, in 1862 the ball was again thrown up in the Market Place. After a promise that in future the game would not be played in the streets of the town, they were let off with costs. After the court case, a handbill copied from the Court Circular was distributed through the town which claimed that the game was started in AD 217.

The proceedings commence with the Important Person plus officials and supporters taking Lunch in the Green Man and Black's Head (which still keeps its name despite the best efforts of the politically correct). These good people very sensibly do not enter the fray. Today the kick-off is at the Shaw Croft; as the Important Person makes his way there the opposing factions sing Auld Lang Syne and the National Anthem. No special abilities or experience are required to fill the post of the Important Person, but a certain agility can be an asset. In 1928 the Prince Of Wales performed this vital function and to commemorate the Royal event two signs have been placed over the doorway of the ginnel through which he proceeded to the 'turning up' of the ball. Keep a look out for these signs next time you are in Ashbourne taking particular note of the grammar.

The teams are lined up on opposite sides of the Henmore stream and the Important Person throws up the ball and heads for safety as fast as his legs will carry him. With

The Green Man and Black's Head.

Prince's Gate, Ashbourne. Note the different ideas on spelling.

ferocious cries of "Down with it," or "Up with it," the teams rush headlong for the ball which disappears under a flailing mass of humanity. So dense is the press of bodies that it is generally impossible to raise a leg in order to kick the ball. Much of the play takes the form of a desperate struggle in the muddy waters of the Henmore Stream with occasional advances as some brave soul charges forwards with ball clutched against his chest until he is overpowered by the opposing forces.

Some claim that there are no rules. This is not so since firearms are definitely banned and teams are expected to bury their own dead. There is no such thing as a foul. Should a goal be scored before 5.30pm, a second ball is thrown up and battle recommences. If neither side manages to score by 10.30pm the police take the ball into protective custody and release it again on Ash Wednesday for the second half. With the game over, all that remains is to go round and collect any arms, legs and other extraneous pieces lying around. What a wonder it is that the poliscoundrels have not seized on some opportunity to ban this harmless game so as to distract the public from their own numerous shortcomings.

Trail Hunting

A pastime which was once very popular was trail hunting with dogs. The races could be over some very wild country, for example right over the summit of Bleaklow. Large wagers were often placed on the outcome, and it was not unknown for the favourite to be 'nobbled' and the event to degenerate into a free for all with the participants slashing at each other with belts and dog leads and even tearing up fences to arm themselves with cudgels the better to draw blood.

The Hare and Hounds in Simmondley village was formerly a starting point for these trail hunts and dogs from all over the country were entered. Presumably the pub got its name for this reason. The landlord from 1859 was Samuel Dewsnap (a good Peakland surname). Samuel trained many trail dogs, but the most famous was a large harrier hunter called Mounter. So successful was Mounter that songs and poems were composed in his honour. Two of the songs are on display in the Hare and Hounds together with a photograph of Samuel Dewsnap.

'Mounter' was of the Harrier breed, out of Mr J. Bennett's 'Bounty' of Simmondley, by Nathan Lee's 'Lincoln' of Newton. (We seem better informed on the ancestry of dogs, than that of human beings) His first appearance in the land of the living was on the 6th August 1879, and he became the property of Mr Dewsnap when he was six weeks old. He was brought up to trail hunting, an exercise he was particularly fond of. He began to show signs of becoming something more than an ordinary dog when he was but a pup. He was entered and won a race among the old dogs at ten months old; at twelve he had gained two first prizes; at two years 18; at three years 33; and eventually at least 50 first prizes were calendared to his credit, second and third honours not counted. He was successful further afield when during Whit-week at

Ulverston near Barrow in Furness in four days he gained two first and two second prizes, although the ground was quite strange to him as he had never been in that part of the country before. The following lines were written in honour of this famous dog:

> With our famous young Mounter none like to encounter,
> The reason is this (so I guess),
> When he's slipped on a trail, he soon shows them his tail,
> For he goes like a London express.

> When following the rag he runs like a stag,
> If it leaves any scent on the ground;
> And with speed and endurance, with perfect assurance,
> His equal has not yet been found.

> When he starts on a hunt he soon shows in the front,
> And it's seldom it ever takes place,
> That he's catch't any more at least not before
> He reaches the end of the race.

> Over inland or moor his footing is sure,
> Up hill, down dale, or on flat,
> And no dog in the race with him can keep pace,
> You may venture to wager on that.

> Over fences he flies, at nothing he shies,
> Through hedges, o'er ditches and rivers,
> Nothing hinders his course, for he goes with such force
> All in front of him trembles and shivers.

> He in Cheshire has run, where a first prize he won,
> When he was only a pup
> And in Lancashire towns he has collared the browns,
> And in Yorkshire he's made them sit up.

> He is Derbyshire bred, and Simmondley fed,
> A credit to the place he belongs;
> His praise we will sing, and his name it shall ring,
> In both recitations and songs.

> He has won fifty races in different places,
> And who knows but he will win fifty more?
> For he's youth on his side, a good dog well tried,
> And he always proves true to the core.

Naked Boy Races

In a 'Brief Historie of Derbyshire,' written about 1665 by Philip Kinder, under the heading Qualitie of People, it says; *'for general inclination and disposition the Peakard and Moorlander (from the adjoining part of Staffordshire), are of the same ayre, they are given much to dance after the bagg pipes, almost every town hath a bagg piper in it. Their exercise for a great part is the Gymnopaidia or naked boy, an old recreation among the Greeks, and this in foot races. You shall have a winter's day, the earth crusted over with ice. Two agonists starke naked runn a foote race for two or three miles, with many hundred spectators and the betts very small.'*

A Mr Forrest gave an eyewitness account of two such races, run in 1755. These were perhaps some of the last to be run since they were discontinued around this time as a result of pressure from the church on the grounds that the sport was barbarous and vulgar. The naked boys races were banned by the High Sheriff in the year 1756 as being indecent. Heavy penalties were imposed on anyone, either taking part or promoting any such sport. Prints and old paintings depicting the race were seized and destroyed and soon the sport became extinct, although races continued for some time in out of the way spots such as Castleton.

Well Dressing

The general consensus of opinion on the origin of the colourful custom of well dressing, or tap dressing as it is occasionally called, seems to be that it dates from pre-christian times and was started by our Celtic forbears when the Brigantes held sway over most of the north of England and worshipped the water goddess Brigantia. The early Christian Church made a practice of taking over pagan sites and customs and may thus have kept this old custom alive. The date of a village well dressing can be fixed like the wakes from the feast day of the patron saint of the Parish Church.

One could easily imagine that in the limestone country that a well which gave year round reliable supplies would be vital to the existence of a village. A few offerings to the Gods might well have seemed a move in the right direction if it would help ensure a regular water supply, but why should the practice be virtually limited to the High Peak? It certainly is not confined to the limestone country since it is carried on, somewhat intermittently, in Charlesworth and Whitfield, hardly districts plagued by drought, and also across the county borders into Cheshire at Gee Cross, and Yorkshire at Penistone. If there was any connection with the shortage of water in limestone country, or with the ancient Brigantes, why is there no trace of the practice further north in the Yorkshire Dales?

Of course it it always possible that folks liked to take any opportunity for a celebration and that blessing the local wells at the Wakes was a part that the local Vicar became involved in. When men first became interested in excavating burial mounds the work was usually under the supervision of some member of the local gentry or the Vicar

Annual Well Dressing, Hope.

Townend Well, Old Glossop.

Mermaid's Pool.

Derbyshire Dewpond, Wardlow.

since these were the only people with the time and money to carry out such studies. Education was essentially based on Christianity at the time so it is hardly surprising that when they discovered anything whose use they could not deduce, it was called a cult object. Whatever the origins of the custom, religious or otherwise, even if you are not a devotee of Brigantia, any well dressing is worth a visit if only to admire the skill of the practitioners of the art.

Wells were a focal point in village life where the women would meet as they went to carry water home and the young men would congregate during the evening. Another very different custom which has no religious connections whatsoever which was once prevalent in connection with village wells was that of throwing strangers into them. If a young man from another hamlet came to court a local girl he might easily end up in the wells. This was a practice which the Derbyshire Constabulary tried to put a stop to in their early days, not always successfully. Certainly within living memory it was said that you were not a Whitfielder if you had not been baptised by being tipped into the Whitfield wells.

With the advent of piped water supplies the sites of many old wells have disappeared but their location is often evident by such names as Fountain and Spring Streets or Wellgate.

The Ebbing and Flowing well lies besides the road through Barmoor Clough roughly opposite the entrance to Bennetston Hall (SK 085797). It was once ranked among the wonders of the peak, the flow of water being intermittent due to the action of a natural syphon. According to Bulmer's Derbyshire it stopped functioning fully at around the same time as the railway was built but as the railway is at a lower level it is difficult to imagine why it should have interfered with the workings of the well. The two events were almost certainly unconnected. It is more likely that in the porous limestone the water found a different route and destroyed the full syphon effect. Around 1948 the level of water could still be seen rising and falling slightly, but it was hardly such a spectacle as to draw vast crowds to see a Wonder of the Peak. Today it is a muddy pool where cows drink.

The Mermaid's Pool on Kinder Scout must have been named by someone with a fevered imagination; no self respecting mermaid would wish to be be seen in such a murky pond which holds no attractions even on the sunniest day.

In the limestone country beside the A623 and in Wardlow there are some fine examples of Derbyshire Dew Ponds. These are shallow saucer shaped depressions lined with concrete which seem always to be full of water. Clearly some is provided by the ample rainfall of the district, but the theory is that they are kept full by water condensing on the cold concrete in the night. There are those who hold that the theory does not work in practice; perhaps one of these experts should make it their business to tell the local farmers because they keep using them.

When you next visit Eyam make it your business to examine the ancient Eyam water supply which is comprised of a series of wells. The wells consist of blocks of millstone grit which have been laboriously cut out by hand. It must have required weeks of work, first to cut out the rectangular block of stone and then carefully hollow it out. The Eyam water supply is of interest for several reasons; firstly the wells were constructed over 400 years ago which must make it one of the oldest examples of a public water supply in the country; secondly Eyam is located on the boundary of the sandstone and the limestone, so that wells in close proximity to one another can supply soft and hard water. Water falling on the permeable sandstone filters its way down until it meets the underlying impervious shale. The sandstone acts as a reservoir for the water which can only exit by a series of springs where the shale is exposed at the surface. Underneath the shale is the thick bed of the limestone which over the centuries has been dissolved by water to leave fissures providing a convenient means of draining excess water from the springs above.

These stone troughs were once to be found at convenient points along the roads to cater for horses and travellers. Many have been destroyed, largely by the action of frost in severe winters and since horse drawn traffic is no longer with us there was no need to repair them. Others have been swept away as the result of road improvement schemes.

When Nan Garlick was the landlady at the Waggon and Horses in Charlesworth, (opposite the toll bar at the end of Woodseats Lane) she had a large stone trough placed outside the door for the benefit of the horses and in the hope that the carters might stop for a drop of something stronger. The overflow was utilised to flush the toilets. The trough is still there, cracked in places, but used for a fine display of flowers.

Stones

The Mermaid's Pool may be a disappointment, but there are a few other curiosities in the area which may interest the serious walker. On the western flank of Kinder Scout at approximately SK 037877 the Dog Stone, the Old Smithy and several grindstones can be found. It is difficult to give an exact location because the mountainside in the area is littered with huge stones which have broken away from the edges above. The area is so rugged that one's attention is usually concentrated on finding a safe place to put one's feet rather than on examining every rock. The Dog Stone is particularly hard to locate because it is a large flat stone standing on edge in an area covered with similar stones. It has the outline of a dog and there are symbols cut into the rock. These appear to read 'She may be small but is of a fine green stone'; an early advertising slogan perhaps.

The Old Smithy is marked on some maps, to the south of Cluther Rocks but is still easily overlooked as it is a ruin with only a few courses of stone still standing. (On the 1881 Ordnance Survey Map it was already named as the Old Smithy). Close to this ruin is a large rectangular slab of millstone grit, about 8 feet by 4 feet and 8 inches thick,

Hall Hill Well, Eyam.

A fine example of a stone trough at Beacom Houses, on Werneth Low.

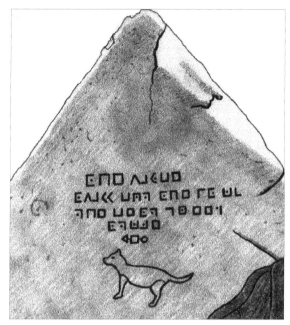

The Dog Stone at Kinder Scout.

Skarratt's Stone, Laund Clough.

with one corner broken off. The interesting feature about this particular stone is that it also has an inscription carved into its under face but the stone has been deliberately placed face down to stop damage to this inscription. If you wish to examine it and attempt to decipher the symbols you had better take along a few sturdy friends.

About quarter of a mile south of the Old Smithy is another very similar ruin which is probably the remains of Sidebottom's Shooting Cabin. It also has a large flat stone nearby. This stone is roughly 4 feet square and has no markings on the underside, so do not do yourself a mischief in attempting to turn it over. Mr Sidebottom's shooting was not restricted to game as the following newspaper extract shows:

Hayfield 12.10.1878: Finding Of A Cannon Ball: Whilst out shooting grouse on Park Hall Moor, Mr Tom Bowden, agent for Mr F J Sumner JP, shot a grouse and when picking it up found a cannon ball of great weight. It is thought to be one fired from a cannon by the late Mr Sidebottom of Broadbottom some years ago as he was in the habit of taking cannon of considerable calibre for practice on the moors around Hayfield.

The grindstones lie scattered on the ground as you make your way downhill from the Old Smithy. Hayfield had a cutlery industry in the 17th century so presumably these few stones are what remains from the days before it died out. They have the appearance of being older than the hundreds which litter the hillside below Millstone Edge near Hathersage. Here perhaps we have an explanation for the existence of the Old Smithy; the chisels and crowbars used in extricating and working the stone would need to be forged and refurbished.

Close to the bottom of Laund Clough (SK 167993), Skarratt's Stone lies about six feet from the stream. The story behind this unusual stone is that a Mr Skarratt became lost on the moors in the area and after wandering for hours sat down on the stone pondering what to do next. Fortunately for him a shepherd appeared out of the mist and guided him to safety. Later Mr Skarratt had his name cut into the stone by a stonemason to mark the spot where he was rescued.

In the Woodlands Valley near Hagg Barn is a stone with the letters of the alphabet cut into it. At one time there were numbers as well, but vandals have smashed this portion off. This stone dates from the days before compulsory education when the building was a Sunday School. In today's jargon, the stone was a visual teaching aid.

The turnpike road from Glossop to Sheffield, the last turnpike built by Thomas Telford and one of the highest in England has been the site of two vicious murders. One was at the aptly named Cut-throat Bridge (SK 212873) where a traveller was done to death in 1635, while the other was commemorated by a stone with MMH (man murdered here) carved onto it. This stone, which is now lost, was set in the dry stone wall beside the road at (SK 071933) just below where it crosses Ramsley Clough. The usual explanation for its disappearance is that the wall collapsed when the snow plough

Cut-throat Bridge on the A57.

Sculpted by the elements - a giant crab's claw near the top of Barrow Stones.

was at work on the road. I remain sceptical of such an explanation; if the heavy stone slab which formed the base of a cheese press could disappear from outside the old pub at Saltersbrook then it would have been a relatively simple matter to move the murder stone in a car boot. Why anyone should want to keep such a memento is hard to understand but then why should someone want to keep a multi breasted stone goddess in a corner cupboard in the house, or a Celtic stone head standing among the broad beans in the hope that they will bear a heavier crop?

At various points on the high gritstone moors there are outcrops of rock which stand out against the skyline. For some reason, walkers seem drawn towards these outcrops; perhaps because many are good points from which to survey the surrounding country, or in inclement weather they can provide a useful shelter from the biting wind and rain. Many are honoured with a name on the map: The Salt Cellar; Coach and Horses; Cakes of Bread; Dish Stone; Boxing Gloves and the Rocking Stones have self explanatory names, and it requires no great flight of imagination as to how the Raven, Crow and others came by their names. Were the Shepherd's Meeting Stones just that and what sad story lies behind the Madwoman's Stones?

Below Wilfrey Edge (SK188955) is a stone with the odd name of Wilfrey Neild. This stone has a hole right through it and the only explanation I can find that makes any sort of sense is that it takes its name from Saint Wilfred's Needle in Ripon Cathedral.

One commemorative stone which remains firmly cemented in place is the one beside the A628 at (SK 038982). The inscription reads "Burned down, two children burned to death aged 3 and 5 years. August 17th, 1858". This is of interest because of the circumstances surrounding the tragedy and the insight it gives into the lives of working people at the time. The Manchester Guardian of Saturday 26th August 1854 gave the following account:

"Sad death of two children. On Monday afternoon last, an inquest was held before before Mr C Hudson at the Black Bull Inn, Tintwistle, on the remains of Joseph Forshaw, aged two years, and Robert Forshaw, aged four years, the children of James and Ann Forshaw, who resided in a hut near the first milestone from Tintwistle, on the Woodhead Road, no other habitations being nearer than 400 yards. The hut in question was only one storey high and was built of rough stones and clay, and covered with straw thatch. It had two rooms, in one of which there were beds for six lodgers, and in the other there was sleeping accommodation for the father, mother and three children. The mother's statement was to the effect that she generally rose at 4.00 a.m. in order that her husband who was a sub contractor under Mr Taylor at the Arnfield Reservoir and the lodgers might go to their work in due time. The children generally rose with her, and after her other boy had gone to his work at the mill she made a practice of going to bed again with the children for about an hour. She had done this on the previous Friday morning, and after rising a second time, she milked a cow and

A fantastic rock formation at Barrow Stones.
This particular tor is worth viewing from almost any angle.

Children burnt to death - a Victorian tragedy at Tintwistle.

occupied herself with other work until between 9 and 10 o'clock. She then went to weed a patch of potatoes close by the house, leaving a fire burning, and the two children asleep in a bed which stood about a yard from the fire. She had been in the potato ground for about an hour, when she bethought herself of going home to the children, but on looking at the house, she saw that it was enveloped in smoke. She unlocked the door and tried to get in for the children, but was compelled to retreat, as the roof was falling in and the place was in flames.

Other witnesses stated that they saw the fire, and went to the place and one of them broke in through the lodgers room but could not render any service as that part was on fire. The children's remains which were found where the bed had stood were drawn from the burning ruins with a potato hoe, their bodies falling to pieces. The beds, furniture, clothes, and other contents of the house were consumed. The jury returned a verdict of accidental death stating at the same time that there had been gross neglect which had been the cause of the accident. The children were interred in one coffin the same evening."

Anyone who thinks they live in difficult and stressful times should read the foregoing from time to time and count their blessings.

Glossop Railway Station has a few features worthy of a second glance. The ticket office window is a masterpiece of beautiful polished wood and just to its left is a fine old red post box with the letters V.R. cast above the letter slot. The line from Glossop to Dinting was built at Lord Howard's expense who was guaranteed 5% interest on his outlay up to £9,000. The contracts for its construction amounted to £6963. This arrangement enabled the line to be built without an Act of Parliament because it was classified as a private line. The line was later sold to the Railway Company at a profit, but Lord Howard retained the use of a private waiting room at Glossop which can be seen immediately to the left of the post box. The doorway has been built up with matching stone.

About a mile north of Peak Forest is Eldon Hill and in its side is the Eldon Hole, once reputed to be bottomless. It is a perpendicular chasm and there was a popular local tradition about an old woman's goose that flew down the hole and after being given up for lost, subsequently emerged at the mouth of the Peak Cavern, at Castleton, over two miles away. It is easy to understand how such a notion gained credence in limestone country where streams can disappear underground to reappear elsewhere, but later explorations showed that there was no other entrance to the hole.

Downstream from the Sheepwash Bridge at Ashford in the Water is another old bridge which carries the following inscription cut into the stonework. M. HYDE 1664; This commemorates a gentleman whose horse shied and threw him into the stream where he drowned. He must have been injured because although the water is fairly deep, a fit man should have been able to wade to the bank without undue difficulty.

Lord Howard's Private Waiting Room at Glossop station.

M. Hyde's Leap at Ashford in the Water.

On the bridge over the Derwent at Cromford yet another leap is remembered by the inscription:

The Leap of R.M. B.H. Mare June 1697

B.H refers to Benjamin Hayward who lived at Bridge House nearby, but the identity of R.M. is a mystery. At this point on the bridge there is a 15 foot drop into the stream, but neither horse nor rider sustained injury.

A Tom Cat With Wings

Here is an extract from the High Peak News; June 25th 1887:-

"The most interesting item in natural history, so far as the Matlock district is concerned, transpired this morning, our reporter learns that Mr Roper, of Winster, while on Brown Edge, near that village, shot what he thought to be a fox, which had been seen in the locality some time previously on Mr Foxlow's land. Thinking he had missed his aim, Mr Roper gave up the quest; but returning later, he found he had killed the animal. It proved to be an extraordinarily large tom cat, tortoiseshell in colour, with fur two inches and a half long, with the remarkable addition of fully-grown pheasant wings projecting from each side of its fourth rib. Unfortunately the climate having been so excessively hot, the animal was allowed to putrefy, and, after being gradually exhibited all round the district, the carcass has now been interred. It was seen by Mr Joseph Hardy and ample witnesses, so that there is no doubt the museums have missed a most curious animal. Never has its like been seen before, and eye-witnesses state that, when running, the animal used its wings outstretched to help it over the surface of the ground, which it covered at a tremendous pace."

This unusual creature is not the only one which has been claimed in the past. Outcrop miners on Gresley Common, Burton on Trent, claimed to have found a live newt in a piece of coal hewn at a depth of 36 feet. The newt was about 6 inches long, had four active legs and a pair of beady eyes. Its breathing was normal, the skin rough and almost black. An extraordinary feature of the specimen was that it had no mouth - only a line was discernible where the mouth should be. The discovery recalls the fact that a few years ago men at Netherseal Colliery - three miles away - claimed to have found a live toad embedded in stone. Both the mouth and the eyes of the toad were sealed, and it lived only a short time after it had been brought to the surface.

When the Mottram Cutting was being driven through to improve the road between Mottram and Stalybridge, workmen found a live toad or frog (opinions differ) inside a cavity in a stone. The stone was set into the wall of the cutting and at one time the shape of the creature could be made out clearly. The stone is still in place but weathering has made the shape indistinct.

Such discoveries naturally arouse suspicions among the scientific community. The difficulty is that we cannot have a scientist to hand every time a miner or quarryman splits a lump of coal or stone, on the off chance that some strange creature may be lurking within. On the other hand it not unknown for workmen to play practical jokes; I well remember when building alterations were being carried out at Wren Nest mill around 1955, that the labourers managed to strike some form of treasure almost every time they stuck a spade in the ground. The odd thing was the rings and coins discovered were remarkably clean with no soil clinging to them.

A True Wonder of the Peak

Just outside the confines of the Peak Park (Robin Hood could have stood atop the grindstone marking the boundary and shot an arrow to the very spot) stood a most remarkable establishment. At a first glance it appeared to be a cafe, but a closer examination revealed a strange state of affairs. Prominent signs were posted announcing that coach passengers, lorry drivers, cyclists and hikers were not admitted. Furthermore, although there was a car park beside the building, access was always prevented by a chain across the entrance and the park was half covered with grass. The wonder was how customers were expected to arrive, just what category of person could actually dine within, and how the proprietor made his living?

The last news I heard of the place was of a visit by a gentleman from Venezuela whose curiosity was aroused when he heard about this odd institution. This foreign gentleman was standing opposite the building when the proprietor rushed out, complete with chef's hat and apron, shouting in an agitated manner, *"What do you want?"*

The Venezuelan was prepared for just such an eventuality and promptly took a photograph and with the words *"Gracias, Senor"* took his departure. Presumably the good folks of Venezuela will look at the photograph and gaze in wonder at a savage inhabitant of the Peak.

A Mystery Solved

From time to time iron balls are unearthed and the finders immediately leap to the conclusion that they have discovered a cannon ball. One gentleman who lived in a former farmhouse in Old Glossop was convinced that his home had been bombarded by Cromwell's troops during the English Civil Wars. The first objection to this theory is that it is extremely unlikely that any cannon ever entered Glossop-dale at that time because there were no roads worthy of the name and the armies in that struggle had the greatest difficulty in moving their artillery on such roads as there were.

The true explanation is much more prosaic; if you examine a few of the 'cannon balls' you will notice that they vary considerably in size. This is because they were once used in ball mills in which they rumbled round and round breaking up the contents into a fine powder and were thus gradually worn down in the process. In the case of the Old Glossop house, the balls had been discovered by local boys and rolled down the hill for a lark, finally ending up in the gentleman's garden. If you do not believe a word it, perhaps I should tell you that one of the culprits is well known to me.

More Research Required

Overlooking Bradwell is a hill known as Rebellion Knoll and there must surely be a good reason for this. The Women's Institute in Bradwell is called the Rebellion Knoll Branch and yet the members do not seem to know the reason for the name, neither do any of the local historians I have questioned; a thorough search of the Local Studies library at Matlock has also drawn a blank. In the Derbyshire Advertiser of September 1924, there was a query from a gentleman seeking information on the origin of the name but it also failed to elicit a reply.

Despite these setbacks I am convinced there is good reason for the name. In 1649 during the troubled times of the English Civil War, 4000 lead miners in Derbyshire were in revolt against the Earl of Rutland, who would not permit them to dig for ore near his house. The miners argued that he was putting his own interest before the interests of the nation and offered to submit their case to the arbitration of the Court of the Duchy of Cornwall, which had jurisdiction in the mining of tin and lead throughout England. The Rump Parliament, however, insisted on dealing with the dispute itself and in due course its committee found against the miners. The miners reacted fiercely. Under the pretext of attending a sporting match, 5000 miners gathered in a rebellious mood, half of them on horseback, armed with pistols and swords. Parliament was ready for just such a contingency and had a regiment of cavalry in readiness who fell upon the miners seizing their horses and swords, forcing them to disperse. The result was that the Derbyshire miners became firm supporters of the Levellers. There were also disturbances by unemployed handloom weavers after the Napoleonic Wars. Either of these incidents could explain the name of Rebellion Knoll.

We should not lose sight of the fact that history is written by the victors and the Establishment has no wish to put the idea of rebellion into people's heads, hence the true account of what has occurred is not always to be found in print, but rather in folk memory.

Ups and Downs of the Peak District

I am indebted to an old copy of the Sheffield Clarion Ramblers handbook for the following descriptions, which might be a good way to finish. A Lincolnshire farm lad obtained a situation in Edale, with a farmer, and wrote home to his father, giving his first impressions of this deep and once very lonely valley. He informed his father; *"You must come over. They've gotten so much land they have to rear it up on end."*

Another description, given by a cattle dealer, when refreshing himself in the old Millstone Inn near Hathersage, was to the effect that when one was walking in the Peak District; *"Yer knees were up ter yer belly, or else yer 'eels were up ter yer arse."*

Follow that!